MORE THAN A JOB?

THE PLAYER'S AND FAN'S PERSPECTIVES

BY ROGER TITFORD *WITH EAMON DUNPHY*

FURTHER THOUGHT PUBLISHING

1992

First published in Great Britain in 1992 by
FURTHER THOUGHT PUBLISHING
Clumber Cottage,
High Street, Upavon,
Pewsey, Wilts., SN9 6EA

A CIP CATALOGUE RECORD FOR THIS BOOK IS AVAILABLE FROM THE BRITISH LIBRARY

ISBN 0-9518771-0 -0

Cover Design
Paul Johnson

Page Design
Sarah Mabbutt

Printed and bound in Great Britain by WM Print Limited, Walsall

Picture Credits:
Cover pictures by kind permission of Reading Evening Post

Front Cover:
Eamon Dunphy scores against Crewe; Friday and Barker look on.

Back Cover:
Clive Thomas (referee) and Tranmere transfixed by Friday's goal.

Robin Friday and young admirers (versus Tranmere).

ACKNOWLEDGEMENTS

Firstly, many thanks are due to Eamon Dunphy for his willing participation in re-living a rather forgotten episode of his playing and journalistic career and for his permission to re-print some of 'The Eamon Dunphy Columns.' Thanks also to Inge Eulitz for her help and hospitality.

Reading Public Library and the Reading Evening Post have been both efficient and helpful. Paul Grantham provided some useful objective recollections from the terrace and Paul Johnson designed the cover. John Bunyard, Andy Lyons, John Gaustad and Stephen Davies all offered useful guidance and comments.

Most of all, Christine King inspired and encouraged the idea to fruition and considerably enhanced her computer skills in the process.

For Christine

INTRODUCTION

The kind of football achievement described in this book is the kind that's customarily easy to ignore or forget. You'll find it on page 595 of the current Rothman's Football Yearbook alongside 120 very similar feats. In the greater scheme of things it's just a statistical dot. But, of course, at the time it mattered hugely to the players and supporters, dominating their lives for the best part of a year.

Yet like almost all those other Fourth Division promotions (and the major portion of all other football played besides) it did not become a famous enough legend to be recorded or re-told. Even the meagre TV footage has been wiped so the tape could be re-used for a piece about getting a cat out of a tree or something. At the end of our day there was joy, but at the end of the decade it's just memories.

This book has two purposes. The first is to examine the memories and inter-relationship of a footballer and a supporter in the context of a season that mattered greatly to both. Memories are crucial to football people. When the anxious hours are long forgotten and the feelings of victory have ebbed away there simply isn't anything else left. That the season in question was fifteen years ago and involved a Fourth Division club, need not, I hope, make it irrelevant or uninteresting. Even if the names mean nothing, the story and the arguments may ring true.

The second objective is to bring to a wider audience and to 'posterity', some of Eamon Dunphy's earlier writing on football. In a sense Brian Glanville inspired this book with his introduction to 'Only a Game?' - Dunphy's diary of half an unsuccessful season at Millwall - which he described as the best book ever written by a professional footballer. He added:

"Let us be grateful for what we have, even if it would have been better to have Dunphy as tyro, Dunphy in his other existences at Manchester United, York, Charlton and Reading."

Well, there was more. After 'Only a Game?' Dunphy did write of better times. Every Saturday for two years, the Eamon Dunphy Column appeared on the back page of the Reading Evening Post.

Encouraged both by Glanville's request and by the re-printing of 'Only a Game?' I set to work, resurrecting those columns and travelling to Dublin to talk to Eamon and to find out what he remembered of and thought of those times now, some fifteen years later.

These columns were excellent material with which to bring back memories and to allow the player and supporter to discuss their, sometimes different, views of the same events. Eamon has kindly given me permission to reproduce a selection of these columns.

There's more of him than me in what follows simply because he's got the more interesting part to play. The reason I'm putting it all together is because it still means something to me but not, as we shall see, to him.

If this slim volume has any claim to originality it is to take the study of the player / fan relationship a step or two further. Apart from the obvious reason, it's called 'More Than a Job?' because professional football to the true fan is just that. The fan imposes certain obligations on the player. It's not just the gate money we invest, it's our hearts too. Originally, as a point of contrast, I put in quite a bit about what I do but I decided to cut it out. It wasn't anything more than a job.

A lot of footballers have written about their livelihood but none more honestly or outspokenly than Eamon Dunphy. In the past five years or so, more and more fans are having their say in print. But never have the player and supporter met before between the same covers. Whilst what you have here is clearly not intended to be representative, perhaps it can be enlightening and bridge-building.

Eamon Dunphy has become more famous as an ex-footballer, certainly in his native Ireland, than he was as a player. He was at Manchester United at the time of Law, Charlton and the young Best, played 23 times for Eire but never fulfilled his ambition of playing in the First Division. The major portion of his career was spent in the Second Division with Millwall. This book deals with the events of Reading's Fourth Division campaign of 1975/6.

After retiring from League football in 1977 Eamon returned to Ireland and linked up with Johnny Giles in an attempt to create a great football club at Shamrock Rovers. He moved into journalism and television, in the sporting and political spheres, and has become a substantial figure on the Irish media scene. In 1987 he wrote the best-selling biography of the rock band U2 and in 1991 published a major biography of Sir Matt Busby, 'A Strange Kind of Glory'.

'Only a Game?' was published in 1976 to much critical acclaim. In 'More than a Job?' we hear a different voice, a voice that Eamon now feels is more truly his own than that in 'Only a Game?'. We have a more rounded picture of a full season, an understanding of how the pro views the structure of the team, the sense of a pro's fear and achievement and the player's paradoxical relationship with his supporters - both needing and rejecting them. Eamon, now, is deeply disillusioned by, and pessimistic about, professional football in England.

Like Eamon nowadays, I myself "err to a Corinthian vision" of the game. Apart from that I am a traditional supporter of my local team.

My roots are strongly intertwined with the club and its immediate neighbourhood. I was born and schooled within sight of the floodlights and brought up about a mile away. My first memory of Elm Park is as a bewildered five year old, lost and alone, thinking I'd stumbled across the Huntley & Palmer's biscuit factory. As I investigated the turnstiles and exits a fat, scruffy old man told me "Clear off out of it." Sometimes I think if only I'd heeded that early warning ......

But four years later, with my Dad for protection, I was back and hooked and since the age of fifteen I have rarely missed a home match. In 1975/76 I was twenty, about the age at which fans are most active, most passionate and most vociferous. Now I'm at the age when my peer group is joining the missing millions and I'm sometimes joining the blanketed few in the stands. For me, token shareholder, very occasional programme contributor and general by-stander, the spell hasn't yet broken. I'm still enthralled, thrilled and angered. I'd miss them terribly if they weren't there.

My views are those of the committed, but questioning, loyalist; Eamon's are those of the transient professional. The central question that emerged during the writing of this book was, to what extent are we in this together? Part Three of this book reflects on that issue.

Part One is the necessary pre-amble for those readers who weren't at Elm Park all those years ago and Part Two contains the Eamon Dunphy columns, our reflections and a factual commentary to put the material in context.

PART ONE: ESSENTIAL READING

PART TWO: THE EAMON DUNPHY COLUMNS 1975/76

PART THREE: ARE WE IN THIS TOGETHER ?

PART ONE

ESSENTIAL READING

The club that Eamon joined

Eamon Dunphy signed for Reading FC on a free transfer from Charlton Athletic on July 1st, 1975. For Dunphy, much troubled by back injury, it was a last chance to continue in league football although it was "a come down" even to play in Division Four again. For Reading, often regarded as one of the duller lower division clubs, it was a glamorous signing. Very few former internationals had found their way to Elm Park over the past decades.

Reading were, and are, a perennial Third Division side neither burdened by great promise nor tarnished by past indignity. But in 1975 they found themselves, still to their great surprise, locked in the Fourth Division, where they had unluckily arrived in 1971.

Since 1972 the manager had been Charlie Hurley, a former Eire international colleague of Dunphy's. It was looking like his fourth and last chance to win promotion for Reading.

In the previous three seasons Reading had finished seventh, sixth and seventh in Division Four without ever seriously challenging in the latter half of the season. In fact it was 50 years since Reading had won their one and only Football League promotion. It seemed that permanently unfulfilled Third Division potential had been replaced by Fourth Division near-misses.

There were good players and talented individuals (not necessarily the same people) at the club but Reading usually lost vital away games. There was no inspirational figure who had been successful either with Reading or another club, someone who knew, by experience, how promotion was won. They lacked real leadership.

Hurley signed three "name" players during that close season: Dunphy - who experienced promotion with Charlton and Millwall (twice), Ray Hiron, a veteran forward from Second Division Portsmouth and Jack Whitham, another forward, with a bitter-sweet career at Sheffield Wednesday, Liverpool and Cardiff.

Hurley was well satisfied with his dealings. "We badly need someone like Dunphy who can put his foot on the ball in the middle of the park. I've got what I want now, the cupboard is full, a squad of 20... I know I have no fairies amongst them. None of them are frightened to go in where it hurts", he told the press.

Who else was in that squad of 20? Eamon found it

easier to remember players than dates, events and results. Some former colleagues came readily to mind, others only after some prompting. By way of introduction, or re-introduction, Eamon recalls the Reading squad of 1975/76 beginning, as would any fan, with centre-forward Robin Friday. (More 'formal' pen pictures are in the Appendix).

"Robin was key to that side", Dunphy remembers. "He was a really talented guy who, home or away wasn't afraid of the game. He could win matches with his physical strength and he had the personality to be bigger than any occasion he had to face. He scored vital goals and he did things when we were struggling that would revive our spirits."

Friday was a one-off, a footballing 'gypsy' whose antics and abilities wouldn't look out of place on the pages of 'VIZ' magazine. He could dribble, he could battle, he could shoot, he could even kiss a policeman after scoring the winner. Mind you, knowing Robin, he'd probably met him somewhere before!

"Everything used to go through Friday", recalls a friend of mine today. "Give the ball to Friday and he'd just do it and he did. The crowd used to go to watch Friday play. He took players on and beat them by pure skill alone. He looked as though he was enjoying it whereas some of the other players, particularly today, look as though they're just doing a job of work. It was infectious and it got to the rest of the team. He certainly had a good rapport with the crowd." On that much the memories of player and fan coincide exactly.

There was also Steve Death, something of a goalkeeping legend. Until very recently the man who has appeared more times than anyone for Reading, and who still holds the Football League record of over 1,000 minutes play without conceding a goal, he was a former England Schoolboys international and was then a vital member of the Reading team.

"Death was a very, very good keeper", claims Dunphy "robbed of his desserts by the perception, or rather the reality, of him being small. One of the best keepers I've ever played with, a terrific presence gave a great sense of calm about him. Very honourable, very straight, very hot-tempered but kept it bottled up. A forbidding man, he took shit from no-one."

There was John Murray, former Burnley and England under 23 forward, who was appreciated on the terraces for a lot of long-range goals and penalties even if his head used to go down quite quickly.

"With Murray", says Dunphy, "it wasn't so much the goals, but the goals helped obviously. He was a luxury item, he scored goals you didn't expect to get. The thing with

Minty was to get him to do the basics right. He was a skilful lad, but you couldn't budget for him. With him it was a question of getting him on the pitch fit, getting him to do the basic things, closing people down, the staple diet of any team. He was never a fit lad, didn't have an awful lot of hunger for the job when the going got tough. If he was a racehorse you'd put blinkers on him. I liked him in the side because he was a skilful player and skilful players make the job easier."

The fan's judgement and memory of a player quite naturally encompasses his whole career at the club whilst the fellow-pro is only interested in the part he played in it. There can be huge discrepancies. Personally, I simply didn't remember anything of Gordon Cumming in mid-field. The Cumming I remember is only associated with the Chappell, Wagstaffs (1970-74) era when he was a good winger. For Dunphy, Cumming was integral . "A very good player - always available, very neat, always made sure the ball went to one of our shirts, very valuable, took a lot of stick from the crowd but that's because they don't understand the game. A good character who wanted to win."

In a sense we're both right. Factually, Cumming played 30 games, scored once, was made captain to add "more aggression" and was promptly sent off twice in the next three matches. Shortly afterwards he was injured, missing the vital run-in to promotion. But it seems a crowd's judgement of a player is made quickly and becomes hard to alter. Cumming was playing a Billy Bremner role but still being judged by the crowd in his 1970 "Willie Henderson surrogate" form.

Dunphy, as we see later, struck a personal bond with Geoff Barker an average, salt-of-the-earth centre-half formerly with Hull and Darlington who, in Eamon's mind, was virtually ever present. In fact he too, like Death, Cumming, and midfielder Bruce Stuckey, all missed the last third of the season. The pro retains only a memory of the 'model' team.

Others, briefly, of that team were young local products Gary Peters and Steve Hetzke in defence, ("Put them together and you got a half-wit, they loved the glory"), with experienced former Portsmouth centre-half Tom Youlden and full back Dave Moreline and Stewart Henderson, (ex-Fulham and Brighton respectively).

Bruce Stuckey, ("We got an awful lot out of Bruce that wasn't really in him. He was a soft lad, a bit of power and pace but you'd have to carry him"), and Bryan Carnaby ("good, honest, just a soldier, frightened to death of the crowd and the ball"), filled in in mid-field.

Up front Ray Hiron was nearly ever present, ("Jesus, I never thought about Ray. It's funny how you don't remember people. He was an irrelevance in many ways, timid, but a good footballer"), Jack Whitham very rarely present, ("He was never fit, Jack, a delicate lad, it'd either happen for him or it wouldn't. Hated muck and bullets"), and there were two transfer deadline signings, Dennis Nelson from Crewe, ("good, pacey, not afraid") and Mick Hollis from Stockport ("kept away from the ball").

Cumming and Barker apart, this fan's memory and judgement matches that of the pro fairly closely. The youngsters, Peters and Hetzke, improved significantly after Dunphy left and are seen now in a better light.

It was a lively and interesting side, "a very good side", recalls Dunphy. "My personal memory is of a happy year. I was made captain and the biggest difficulty I had was keeping Minty Murray and Robin Friday on the straight and narrow. Minty liked a jar and Robin liked everything he could get his hands on. I spent quite a bit of time stopping them getting drunk before the game and then getting drunk with them afterwards."

As for Dunphy himself, I remember quite clearly him being in the side and doing some clever things from time to time but not as a dominating individual. With his established reputation and his old-fashioned inside-right's build I think we always expected a bit more than perhaps the Fourth Division, even in those days, was prepared to allow.

So, on paper Reading looked a good pre-season bet for promotion, (on paper they usually did). Former goalkeeper Mike Dixon said, "I shall be very surprised if they don't get out of Division Four this year."

Fans felt that with the players and financial resources available, (compared to the Workingtons, Newports and Southports), the club ought not to be in Division Four - but they felt that way for the last four seasons too and they had always been disappointed.

Who else would be in the frame? Huddersfield would be playing in Division Four for the first time ever and keen to end the humiliation of being a division below Halifax. Watford had an expensive collection of skilled veterans. Graham Taylor had pushed Lincoln to within a last match whisker of promotion the previous season, while Ron Atkinson was doing good things at Cambridge. Bournemouth had a promising young side with Kevin Reeves at centre-forward. But there were also a dozen sides you could just forget about - eternal Northern chopping blocks who'd turn up in faded red strips, go two down and pack in.

The Reading Evening Post concluded, almost despairingly, "They must surely have a good chance this time round."

Outstanding memories and silly mementos

Years later it seems memories condense in to a powerful vision or story for a particular season. Eamon and I pondered the question - What's the first thing that sticks out when you try to remember that season?

For me it was one outstanding game against Tranmere Rovers in late March. Tranmere were third, Reading were fourth and Huddersfield fifth, with games in hand. Reading hadn't played well for three months and now was the time they had to deliver. Too many times in the past Reading had failed in similar fixtures.

We had to win that game to prove we were good enough. Before that no-one believed Reading were good enough. It was make or break that night.

I remember feeling tense about that match all week, a different kind of tension from Cup-ties when you've either done it or you haven't and there's no use crying over spilt milk. I also remember feeling we never did that well against Tranmere. It was a fine night and the biggest crowd of the season so far was there; 10,961 - including many from Merseyside. One of them, bizarrely, was playing cards with my mum when I finally got back from the pub that night.

We were brilliant. Clive Thomas gave us a kick-start awarding two first half penalties. They were penalties but not the sort you usually get, outside the referees association exam room. Then Robin got his goal; probably beat a couple, certainly turned, volleyed a shot into the top corner from twenty five yards. I can't quite remember but I did order the press photo ... which showed two Tranmere defenders staring, wide-eyed and transfixed, at their own goalmouth while Clive Thomas had his hands on his head in amazement rather than pointing back to the centre spot, (see back cover). Friday got another, Murray completed his hat-trick for 5-0 and we knew then we were ("probably") going up. We didn't think Tranmere would recover but they did and went up in fourth place. I'd been watching Reading for twelve years at that point and I'm sure it's the first time I'd ever left Elm Park thinking 'yes, we are going up this time.'

Eamon knew that defeatist mentality. It was the first thing he recalled about that season.

"There was a great sense of Reading never having got promotion for fifty years and the weight of that got heavier as we got nearer. Charlie Hurley had had several goes at it and one of the things I remember most was the scepticism in the town. Whilst in the early stages it didn't matter to us, it didn't affect us, in the later stages it began to eat away a little bit at us."

His principal feelings for Reading FC are not so much to do with the promotion season but what immediately followed and coloured the whole experience. He and Cumming led a pay revolt in protest at the terms they were offered. On the first day of the next League season Dunphy was given a free transfer. Now, proudly, he claims the world's earliest free transfer - despite which he went on to play another 31 games for the club in Division Three.

One particular experience symbolised his memory of life at Reading:

"There was a guy who'd been a supporter of the club for 50 years and he offered to give us a cow, which he'd have slaughtered and we'd get loads of meat and stuff if we got promotion, and that was a great attraction because we weren't getting enough money at Reading. They were never profligate."

"We got promotion and the man duly provided the heifer or whatever it was. We all went to Reading market, with the help of a local butcher to select an appropriate victim. We were photographed with the poor fellow stroking its head like signing its death warrant."

"A couple of weeks elapsed, we'd all dispersed for the summer. The news came through that the beast had been slaughtered and we could come to Reading and collect. On the day of sale the butcher said you should get 230lbs of meat, between about sixteen players and we decided to add Charlie Hurley and Maurice Evans and the two lads who did the ground. Split twenty ways, about 10/11lbs each. When we got the plastic bags, which Charlie handed out in the office, we got 5lbs of meat each and it was all the rubbish, no sirloin, no best end, no fillet - all mince and bad meat."

"We were so incensed at the cheapness of it some of the lads refused to take it. This was our simple little perk. You don't get free meat, you don't get much at all as a Fourth Division footballer. It was so petty to get it filched from under our noses by people who weren't without. This happened in the middle of the wages row and the lads were soured in a terrible way, after we'd had a good year."

As a fan you just sit back and think what a bloody sad memory to keep. Of course it wasn't really about who got sirloin and best end, but who got reward and respect. With morale and relationships like that it's no wonder that eight months later 'The Brisketmen' were bottom of the Third Division, Hurley was out of a job and the previous season, to all strategic intents and purposes, had been a waste of time. Meanwhile you, the fan, have spent your time and money unquestioningly and unwittingly supporting them up and down the land. Ouch.

Was there anything more tangible to be had at the end of the day, as they say, than five pounds of brisket? Well, you get nothing from the League for finishing third in the Fourth Division so it's up to each to collect his own silly mementos of great times.

Eamon Dunphy, alas, was a non-starter in this game. "I've got nothing, absolutely nothing from any stage of my career. I regret the fact I haven't got a single programme, it's dreadful. I was stupid not to keep them. It was the most important, challenging time of my life but at the time I was pre-occupied with the job in hand."

Some members of the family have a Dunphy Eire international shirt and the only memento of his club career is a picture of Eamon and Stewart Henderson embracing after a Reading goal that hangs, I'm told, in his daughter's bedroom.

"There's something transient about the life of a pro footballer, you live for the moment, take the moment and look for where you get the next one. It's survival and you don't have time to savour or treasure."

Not so the football fan. As a hoarder by birth and historian by education I've got programmes, pictures, my own photos, souvenir newspapers and the Eamon Dunphy columns and am therefore too odd to count for anything. For the typical fan there isn't too much to keep. "Probably the programmes", thought a friend and supporter of my age. "That's about it. I've got all the Reading programmes from 1965 to 1978. I haven't bought one for seven or eight years. I looked at those programmes not long ago actually - from the point of view of selling them in a car boot sale but I decided not to." Thus a middle-aged married man with two kids keeps in touch with the glories of 1975/76.

Over in Dublin the retired pro has only faded and sometimes false memories. But they are interesting, of different things and tell a fuller story.

PART TWO

THE EAMON DUNPHY COLUMNS 1975/76

The Eamon Dunphy columns and the 75/76 story

Much of the story of the season is told in the following 24 extracts from the Eamon Dunphy columns; the rest is memories, debate and the bits that weren't fit to print at the time.

'Only a Game?' had already been written when Eamon Dunphy joined Reading in July 1975. He'd also had previous experience of writing a weekly column in the South London Press so the Reading Evening Post regarded him as something of a coup.

"Eamonn Dunphy. Eire international and former York City, Millwall and Charlton player, who has joined Reading this season, is a noted writer on soccer. His weekly comments on the game will appear every Saturday." (For some reason Eamon sprouted an extra 'n' for the duration of his playing career in England).

For Dunphy the column was a significant step in his writing career. 'Only a Game?', he felt by 1990, hadn't truly been his 'voice'. What he wrote in the Post had been truer to himself in tone.

"It was an important period for me as a journalist, to try and find my voice. I'm very grateful to the Post for that and for taking my stuff. The best relationship I had with the people of Reading was through that column rather than through my efforts as a footballer. I was able to communicate to them something of what it was like to be a footballer."

"Temperamentally, I was one for blurting things out. There were obviously things you couldn't say but you had to give a taste of what it was like. It gives a little sense of the characters involved."

Typically Eamon had not kept a copy of any of these columns. What does he think of them now?

"I think it's a bit twee compared with the journalism I went on to afterwards but then you are severely constrained about writing about the team you are playing in. It's nice, gentle stuff. I'm quite pleased with it now. I thought I might be embarrassed by it but I'm not."

Some weeks the column did not even mention matters at Elm Park. These have been omitted. Those that are re-printed have been so in their entirety and touch on matters as diverse as Fiona Richmond and 'Foul'. (the first alternative football paper). Typographical errors have been corrected and the headlines are mine rather than The Evening Post's. Otherwise, that's what the man wrote.

The first column appeared two weeks before the big kick-off and finds Eamon in a coy but optimistic mood.

THE BOYS ARE FIT AND RARIN' TO GO, REALLY

EVENING POST, 9 AUGUST 1975

Despite the acres of space that newspapers devote to pro football I find that very little of the game's real atmosphere is captured by the Press.

This is particularly true of "star" columns that purport to take the reader "inside" the dressing room.

Instead of meaningful comment one is more likely to find players life-styles are covered "in-depth".

Boutiques, cars, houses and holidays are discussed - some newspapers even carry sexy pin-up photos of hairy-chested players.

The game and the people in it have suffered from its projection in the media. Real drama of what is an exciting and challenging life is obscured behind a smokescreen of phoney "bust-ups" and triviality.

So whilst occupying this page I shall endeavour to spare you from the sales figures for my new boutique, the performance of my "Jensen Interceptor" and the only time I'll pose nude is when we win promotion.

I will try also to avoid the banal "The boys are fit and rarin' to go" type comment and instead try to convey some of the passion and enjoyment I and most players get from the game.

INSULT

If you disagree with what I have to say at least I won't insult your intelligence.

Having said all that let me tell you: "The boys are fit and rarin' to go". The snag is that after pre-season training so are all the players at 91 other League clubs.

This is a glorious time of year for all footballers. The weather is beautiful, the atmosphere of a pre-season training camp is relaxed and cheerful.

No teams have been picked so nobody's been dropped yet, no games played, none lost. Last season's failures are cast from your mind; those stupid passes, the goals you missed or gave away might never have happened.

Never again, you say to yourself, not this year... and of course the benign atmosphere around you does nothing to discourage such thoughts. The euphoria that infects the pre-season training camp can be very misleading.

WORRIER

You forget how in April, tired and disillusioned, you were glad to get away from football. The guy you couldn't stand last season doesn't look so bad now, he's in good spirits too.

Even managers have been known to smile in pre-season.

I remember an old manager, one of the world's greatest worriers.

During the season he was permanently on edge, tight-lipped, face drawn, a walking nervous breakdown.

Yet pre-season he was a different man. He smiled, joked with the lads. He strode across the training ground, confident that this year he'd got it right.

He never did, but for him like the rest of us, June and July were good months for dreaming.

Age and experience have taught me to be wary of pre-season and dreams. Yet I must confess I feel that glow of anticipation again as this season draws near.

If you're of a cynical turn of mind stop reading here - for this is where I won't surprise you.

I think that we will win promotion this season.

EQUIPPED

I've been wrong before, but I've also been right, and although there are no certainties in football I think it is undeniable that we are better equipped than most to go up.

Skill, determination and team spirit abounds in this club. In terms of skill this group of players compare very favourably with the Charlton side that last year won promotion to the Second Division.

There is strength in depth too. With 20 good players competing for places, getting into the side will in itself be an achievement.

In the promotion race strength in depth is important in order to prevent complacency and to cover for the inevitable injuries.

A happy dressing room is also very important. It is quite common to find that good team spirit exists in the lower divisions and Elm Park is no exception. At this level of the game egos tend to be smaller than they are in the First Division.

Perhaps the thing that's struck me most about this club is the determination of everybody to win promotion THIS SEASON.

As I have said before, this is the time of year for self-delusion. But this is patently not true in our case.

The evidence of recent years shows that Reading are always a force to be reckoned with in the Fourth Division.

The lessons of recent campaigns, plus the addition of quality players Ray Hiron and Jack Whitham should, *combined with the added determination, leave no room for error this time.*

I'm certain it's going to be a great season and a tough one. Promotion is not easily gained. You have to keep the momentum going for 46 games over nine months. Along with ability, determination and team spirit the most vital ingredient is belief. You've got to believe, that's what will carry you through the difficult days and there will be plenty of those.

An important element in a successful club is its relationship with the supporters. I would go so far as to say that without the right relationship it is impossible to achieve anything.

Good teams don't necessarily win things - good clubs do. The test of a club is what happens day in day out. It all adds up to the end result on Saturday.

During the week the manager, coaching staff, groundsmen, tea ladies, directors and secretary all make a contribution to success.

On Saturday it's the players turn and equally important it's the time supporters too can play their part.

It's YOU who watch who set the scene, create the atmosphere and give the game meaning.

The right kind of support can lift players particularly on bad days. It can make the difference between success and failure. Points are won and lost depending on how the supporters react.

This will be a challenging, exciting year for this club. If you come, be a part of it... the good times and the bad and I'm certain we will make it.

After all, you can't be cynical all your life!

At the time I felt Reading would inevitably get promotion one day but equally inevitably that it would never quite be this season. Looking back, Eamon was more sure of his destiny.

"I was very confident. It didn't take much imagination to see they only needed a bit more. Hiron and myself were 2nd Division players."

"We had a lot of experience, a lot of skill, we needed the mentality factor to harmonise all of that into a side that goes out with the right attitude. That attitude isn't to do or die but to fight the thing on your terms and to dominate the opposition. We established that quite early on as a group of guys."

"Charlie talked about the game as if it was an SAS course, we've got no fairies and all that, and it isn't. It's about intelligence and resources."

Reading's pre-season programme went quite well, which is usually a bad omen. On Saturday before the season began they travelled to nearby non-League Wokingham Town and won comfortably, 2-0.

THE FIRST GAME IS SYMBOLIC

EVENING POST, 16 AUGUST 1975

A day of rest after the Wokingham game. Although we won the game I can remember very little about it. I'd spent Friday night in the bathroom having caught a bug that played havoc with my bowels.

After a sleepless night I felt pretty rough on Saturday morning and thoughts of my pre-match scrambled eggs did little to cheer me up.

The question was, should I play? I didn't feel like getting up, much less playing. What should I do?

Should I : (a) stay in bed and get my wife to 'phone the club, (b) go to the game tell the boss I'd had an uncomfortable night and go out and have a go, (c) say nothing just go out and play.

SNAG

Option (a) seemed sensible (and attractive), but there was a snag! Suppose I stayed in bed, the lads went out and beat Wokingham 6-0, my replacement scored two goals and had the proverbial "blinder".

What would happen to me? I might find myself spending a few more Saturdays in bed!

Option (c) was out - I don't like to suffer in silence - well do you? Also as there was a good chance that I would perform pretty poorly, I wanted an alibi.

So, motivated by man's first instinct, I opted for course (b).

I went to the game, broadcast loudly the eventful happening of Friday night, establishing a cast-iron alibi.

The interesting point of these revelations is: What would I have done if I had been certain of my place in the first team, if we had not had a strong talented squad of players available, a number of whom could fit quite neatly into my No 10 shirt?

AFFORD

You see the sensible, convenient, comfortable thing for me to have done would have been to stay in bed. But that little bit of pressure - the possibility that I could lose my place - meant that I had to push myself beyond what was comfortable and convenient. In other words I couldn't afford to be complacent.

There is no comfortable, convenient way to succeed in football. Complacency can undermine the efforts of an otherwise successful club.

But as my example shows, the existence of a strong

squad can check any tendency towards complacency.

Incidentally, it can also prevent other well-known football ailments such as the "slight pull" or the "mystery injury" which stop you training on horrible January mornings.

Even the "bad cold" can be cured by the existence of able deputies. (Have we at last found a cure for the common cold?).

MONDAY

The week before the season starts - a special time. The pulse quickens, tension in the air, Saturday and Rochdale come sharply into focus.

Rationally the Rochdale game is just one of 46 but psychologically it's very important.

A good result reinforces the pre-season optimism.

A bad result can be shattering, bringing the ghosts of previous failures back to haunt you.

The first game is symbolic, an indicator on which we place too much emphasis. That at least is the rational view.

But as Saturday approaches and one's heart begins to beat quicker, rationality disappears and romance takes over.

Football, the challenging, romantic nine months ahead is inherently irrational and that's what's so marvellous about it.

TUESDAY

A full scale practice game this morning at the Adwest training ground. The side for Saturday has not been named yet, so we line up as 'probables' and 'possibles'.

It's always better to be a probable but of course the possibles are keen to become probables so these games are invariably keenly contested.

If you are a certainty, and there are always some of them, there's not so much pressure. On the other hand if you are a "dodgy probable" like me, these games can be hell.

In the event it was enjoyable, the probables won (with the aid of a hotly-disputed penalty). The ref, usually the boss, has often been accused of favouring the probables. There is absolutely no truth in this!

I remained a probable and although my ambition is to become a certainty I fear I could in time become a possible (impossible). I hope you followed all that!

WEDNESDAY

A nice break in routine today, when we trained at Greenham Air Base.

The Americans are incredibly hospitable, and apart from the superb facilities available for training, they do a great lunch with such pre-inflation delicacies as beef, prawns and turkey, not to mention jelly, cakes and ice cream. Yes it's a hard life!

THURSDAY

We spent the morning on perfecting our set-piece moves.

Over 40 per cent of all goals now come from set-pieces. Organisation and logic can be applied to set-pieces in a way that's impossible with free play.

Ideally everyone should have a function and be collectively tuned in on the same wave-length.

Our session was thorough and this will be a crucial area for us this season.

I remember a previous manager of mine setting up what he considered to be the perfect defensive wall. It was an elaborate and lengthy exercise at the end of which, satisfied, he invited anyone who cared to breach his proud invention.

Up stepped a wily midfield player who promptly curled the ball round the wall into the far corner. Collapse of session, much talk of "smart-arsed bigheads".

FRIDAY

Tomorrow the first game. For the next nine months our lives are dedicated to the business of winning games.

But tonight is a special night for football people.

Kids lie restless dreaming of the conquests their team will make tomorrow.

Their dads, pints in hands, talk cynically in pubs: "They will be just as useless this year".

But in a small corner of their hearts, they too nurture a dream that this will be "our year".

More than anyone the pro dreams tonight. He is more than a dreamer, he is the dream maker.

No matter how long you've been in the game, how cynical you've become, tonight you push the past and the present behind to dream of the future, which for us is nine months long.

Let's hope they're good times.

"The first game of the season is symbolic because it's the first test of your new dream and if it goes very badly wrong then it becomes a test of your character to see if you can survive that. You're never sure your collective character can survive. It can take you a month to recover if you lose badly," explained Eamon.

"You're talking about failure, guys who'd failed all their lives. Failure compounds itself and becomes a monstrous ghost lurking in the back of your head. The collective failure of the past. It isn't just you've lost one match, but that you believe yourself to be a failure with a collection of guys like those at Reading. You don't want to resurrect old ghosts by losing the first match. It's a big deal."

For the fan too the first game is an omen. Being optimistic by nature you want to see how far into the autumn you can keep an unblemished record. A win on the first day represents a still flawless and perfect season. When, a decade later, Reading won their first thirteen matches the Third Division table became a thing of breathtaking beauty, the triumph of perfect form over peremptory chance.

Dunphy's division of the team not by their outfield positions but by the categories certainty, probable and possible is not one that necessarily occurs to fans. The player has to both assess the team collectively and from his individual standpoint. For the fan, unless she's the player's mum too, judgements and loyalties are simpler.

"Players go through emotional stress because their lives, their whole esteem is bound up in whether they're in the team or not. If you're a pro footballer and you're not playing you're literally nothing, you don't exist."

" Is there any altruism in it, that you want to do well for the supporters, so step out of the team to let somebody better in?" I enquired naively.

"No, you don't have that perspective at all. Primarily you're a professional footballer and it's about you. Secondly, linked closely, is the team, because without the team you can't prosper. After that nothing else matters, supporters or the club, doesn't really matter. It's you and those set of guys. It's not the last team that Reading had, and the next team that Reading will have, it's the team you played in that matters and that's where your loyalties lie. You don't have a club perspective and you don't have a fan perspective because your life is too full of harsh realities, and they're bloody harsh, and that's what you have to deal with. In that sense you think no further than your own conditions and they are umbilically linked to the fortunes of your own team."

On that first day of the season in 1975 fortune smiled probably more on Reading than any other team in the League. As Charlie Hurley put it in a somewhat understated manner in the following game's programme notes, "As planned, our set piece was done well although we needed a certain amount of luck for it to count."

THE GOAL THAT NEVER WAS

EVENING POST, 23 AUGUST 1975

No matter how hard you work, how well you plan, or how talented your team, fate will not be denied.

That is both the frustration and the fascination of sport.

The bold facts of the past week - that we defeated Rochdale with the aid of "the goal that never was" and lost to Gillingham by virtue of an "own goal" are deceptively simple.

For those of us who live by the width of a crossbar or the quirk of a ref the week was terrifyingly familiar.

Take Rochdale for example. For six weeks in pre-season training they had worked hard, driving their bodies to fitness, perfecting their tactical planning and on the fateful day had every reason to be pleased with the way things were going.

STRONGEST

They come to Reading, one of the Fourth Division's strongest sides, and do well for 10 minutes.

Then there's a free-kick against them. The kick is taken, the ball crashes into the side netting, the ref awards a goal. Tragedy! - it can't be true! Alas it is.

The first goal of the season is always the most painful concession, but this way it's unbearable.

Yet, how well they took it.

Stunned, helpless, appealing looks. Could it be true - it was.

I couldn't believe my eyes when the ref pointed to the centre circle. Instinctively I accepted an amazing stroke of good fortune and back I hared into position for the restart.

PLEADING

As I stood there waiting for the game to resume I caught the eye of Dick Mulvaney, Rochdale's veteran mid-field player.

He was silently pleading with me "Tell him, tell the ref he's made a mistake."

I looked back, "Sorry Dick I'm not telling."

He didn't expect me to, he wouldn't have.

Still it made me think for a moment. Should I own up?

I quickly dismissed the thought and got on with the game. On the train home I thought about the incident. How should one respond to such a situation? It's a bit like finding a fiver in the street. Does one hand it into the nearest police station?

It's an absolute certainty that we will be on the wrong end of some diabolical decisions before the season ends, but we won't be able to change them. Nobody will "own up", we'll just have to accept them.

A parallel situation in cricket involves the batsman who refuses to walk. Ian Chappell, the Australian skipper is on record as saying he wouldn't "walk".

Ray Illingworth has said that in county cricket he would "walk" but not in a Test match against the Aussies, because they don't.

So it seems the rules of modern sportsmanship, although unwritten, are understood. All depends upon the prevailing mood.

The professional sportsman sees himself as being constantly at the mercy of fate of which referees and umpires are a part.

If fate, the ref, or the umpire should smile at you, well, accept it. The grand gesture so beloved by the amateur no longer has a place, it seems.

Although it saddens me that sport is less gracious than it might be I can't afford that kind of self-indulgence.

I wonder what you feel? I would like to hear from you if you have strong views. But first a question. What would you do if you found a fiver in the street?

FATE

Having smiled on us last Saturday, fate turned her back on us on Wednesday in the League Cup.

We deserved to win the Gillingham game, yet an own goal, missed penalty and some desperate defensive work denied us our "just" rewards.

So much for justice. Anyone who has been in this game for long sometimes doubts the term "just reward".

Still, it's been a good week. Some good fortune, some rough justice, two beautiful League points, a cruel own goal, the heartening support of our crowd.

We are in effect a new side with four new players gradually adjusting to each other and seeking the right blend.

I thought we played better on Wednesday than we did against Rochdale.

At times in the Gillingham game we really began to string our passes together and moved forward with power and purpose. In neither game have we conceded much defensively but the real test of teamwork is in attacking play.

It is a question of rhythm, of knowing where your colleagues are almost without looking.

It takes time to develop, but it's a good feeling when it's there and at times on Wednesday it was.

After Crewe today we go on to Gillingham on Monday optimistic, dreams intact, relieved to have fought real battles, spilt some blood, and survived.

Away games provide a different kind of test. It will be interesting to see how we do. I'm looking forward to it.

Everyone who saw that game against Rochdale will remember 'the goal that wasn't'. I remember the crowd were laughing, not mistakenly cheering a goal.

The Reading players wandered sheepishly back into their own half. Today Dunphy remembers the story slightly differently - and has dined out on this version for years.

"As we ran back I got a guilty conscience. I went to the ref and told him it didn't go in. The lads went 'fuck off', we don't do that sort of thing and the ref would have none of it. I'm sure I told the referee. That column stuns me. I was trying to make a point about ethics in sport. I remember saying that wasn't a goal. I would have thought I had written the column that way."

Wishful thinking or perhaps the ambivalence about speaking out that afternoon still persists.

"I hated that cavalier attitude then. I've got more respect for it now. It was that side of the pro footballer I was anxious to convey to the public - the difference between us and the Henley Rowing Club."

It depends on your attitude, or whether you think a moral victory is worth anything in the long run. I won't forgive Maradona his 'hand of God' goal even if Shilton and other professionals who, in that apt phrase "live by the width of the cross bar" can. The difference, perhaps, is that an amateur has to be friend, neighbour, customer or supplier after the match. His whole person, not just his footballing side, is on display.

The pro resolves his dilemma by absenting himself from moral choice - leaving it all to fate. He'd have some support for that view on the terrace too. Other fans realise it can't always be the case that we're either 'lucky' or 'robbed' and that we never rob others or are unlucky ourselves. In the debate between the professional and the supporter it is a subject that recurs.

THE TEAM IN BLACK VELVET SUITS AND SUEDE JACKETS

EVENING POST, 30 AUGUST 1975

Euston Station 10.30 Saturday morning and we're waiting for Robin Friday. He's a great lad but time keeping is not his outstanding quality.

As we both live in London I'm the one who suffers from his lapses.

"What train are you catching tomorrow?", he says every day.

"The 8.45", says I.

"Great, see you in the buffet" he says deadpan.

He's never on it. He doesn't say "good morning" any more - just "Sorry, mate."

STYLES

10.40... he arrives looking like an altar boy in his new black velvet suit.

"Doesn't he look nice" we all jeer, although looking round we're not exactly soccer's best dressed team.

Ray Hiron has his gamekeeper's jacket on, Steve Hetzke his Chelsea Girl belt, Andy Alleyne his C&W boots, and "Minty" Murray has THAT suede jacket on (again).

We are catching the 11 o'clock train, the miracle of Inter City reducing to two hours a journey that used to take two days - by stage coach - when Ray Hiron first played.

Clothes and age are subjects that provide for much banter among footballers, particularly on Saturday mornings when some light relief is needed.

On the train Robin, Tom Youlden and myself discussed the Saturday morning blues.

The symptoms we all share were aches and pains, drowsiness and feeling generally irritable.

TENSION

It seems inevitable that tension will be around on Saturday mornings and most players agree that these are the worst hours of the week.

As the miles flash by we spend the time reading the papers or pestering the waiter to find out what time we're eating.

Surprisingly nobody is playing cards, a traditional way of passing time on long journeys. Games range from the relatively harmless like "Hearts" and "Solo" to the more expensive "Brag" or "Pontoon".

At Charlton we played a particularly vicious variation of pontoon called "Shoot". So unsuccessful was I that when I left the club the lads considered demanding compensation.

At York we were too poor to play, but at Manchester United things went to the other extreme with so much money changing hands that Sir Matt Busby had to stop card playing.

That was in the days when players were earning £30 a week. Strangely the higher paid modern day player, is far less likely to throw his money around in this way and thankfully big money card schools have disappeared.

Back on the train it's time for lunch - tea, toast and boiled chicken on the menu for us.

STUDY

Meal times provide an excellent study of how behaviour patterns change when one is in a group. Travelling alone I'm offered the toast basket politely and almost tentatively I reach out to take a slice.

Travelling with the team I subject the toast basket to assault and battery. In go the hands (plural), out come three or four slices. "Got any more butter mate?"

The boiled chicken was delicious and there was much undignified scrambling to claim Tommy Youlden's unfinished leg (Robin won).

By now we've reached Stafford where Jack Whitham joins us. He's wearing his "safari suit", a blue denim job that takes a fair bit of stick and takes the heat off Robin.

I think Jack definitely won the sartorial prize.

1.15... we arrive at Crewe. It's what one imagines a typical Crewe day - overcast with a hint of rain.

1.30... inspect the pitch which is small and whilst standing reflect that in recent years the club hasn't done particularly well there.

Back to the dressing room which could be described by an imaginative estate agent as quaint.

A POINT

Still as we begin to concentrate on the game and the adrenalin starts to flow comfort becomes irrelevant.

It turns out to be quite a game, at once heartening and frustrating. Heartening because we showed courage in fighting back from 1-3, frustrating because although we were clearly the better side we failed to win.

We allowed them three soft goals and despite our superior technique, our massive territorial advantage, in the end we were happy to settle for a point.

In football as in all games - in the final reckoning it's not how but how many.

Still it was an away point and not to be scoffed at. Meanwhile I had my own problems. I'd spent the final 15 minutes hobbling on the left wing having strained a hamstring muscle.

I've never had a hamstring injury before. I was alarmed to hear people talk of a three to four week recovery period. As it's turned out it's not that serious but at the same time I felt a bit sorry for myself.

At best I'd miss Monday's League Cup game at Gillingham. At worst I could find myself back with the possibles.

However the sight of the Post's David Dibben at the bar after the game was cheering. We knew we'd done well when "Dibbs" stood us all a drink! (and he hardly moaned at all).

As this is a family newspaper I won't go into detail about our trip home.

What I can say is that we had a nice packed meal, drank a few lagers and had a very interesting conversation with two Swedish nurses.

It says much for the much maligned Scandinavian sense of humour that they managed a conversation in "pidgin English" (ours - they spoke perfect English) with 12 "tired and emotional" footballers.

Unfortunately what the Swedish nurse said to the Fourth Division footballer must remain a secret!

PROOF

I missed Gillingham last Monday, but with Charlton winger Colin Powell I went along to watch.

I've been telling him what a good side we are and if he thought it was all blarney Monday's game proved my point.

The lads were brilliant. It was the best display I've seen from an away team for years.

Yet because of a momentary defensive lapse we only drew.

My only regret was that I wasn't playing. As the final whistle blew a convinced Colin Powell turned to me and voiced what was very much on my mind "How are you going to get back into that team?"

It was a good question.

So, although we are out of the League Cup we have learned much from the experience, mainly that we have a very good side even by Third Division standards.

CERTAIN

People sometimes think it rash to talk of certainties in football - I disagree - I think we are certain to gain promotion.

The biggest sin in my book is to sell yourself short.

This is often the case, particularly in the lower divisions and, dare I say it, in Reading where they've waited 50 years to win something.

Bill Shankly had it right when he said "The two best teams in England are Liverpool and Liverpool Reserves."

We are no Liverpool but neither should we be too modest.

In terms of individual skill and as a team I think we could hold our own in the Second Division now.

In saying so I'm sticking my neck out, but what the hell, I believe events will prove me right.

In today's club blazer, blue tie, grey slacks era it's hard to believe they let them out dressed like that. I do remember seeing the team once lined up in the checkout queue at a motorway service station, making a terrible row. Charlie Hurley stood at the till fiercely peeling from a wad of pound notes. He looked like Charlie Endell (Iain Cuthbertson) from the 'Budgie' TV series, not at all enjoying himself, in his big overcoat, supervising his own shrieking flock of "Budgies". They didn't look at all ready and willing for a post-match discussion with us.

"We were frisky", recalls Dunphy. Sadly what the Swedish nurse said to the Fourth Division footballer must remain lost to posterity. Eamon can't remember.

Coming from 1-3 down to draw at Crewe was a crucial early season pointer. Reading won their next home game against Southport 1-0, with Eamon Dunphy on the sub's bench, replaced by wide midfield man, Bruce Stuckey. An unchanged team visited Lincoln in what was to be an important match.

To those listening at home on the radio it was, nevertheless, a disappointing result. Ever prepared to judge on the last result, it seems like the same old hype, the same old con. Two years before, we were unbeaten for the first nineteen games and still didn't go up so this was hardly encouraging.

THE LOSERS' DRESSING ROOM

EVENING POST, 13 SEPTEMBER 1975

SATURDAY

Ten o'clock on King's Cross Station - a bit early for humour but Ray manages to get a laugh.

He's done it again - this time it's an ancient blue blazer with PFC on the pocket. "You've really raided the wardrobe this time," laughs Robin.

Ray, good humoured as ever, begins to explain the garment's history. The initials, he tells us, stand for Portsmouth Football Club.

"Are you sure the 'P' doesn't stand for 'Pensioner' Ray." Robin again. Never mind Ray.

I can't wait to see what he takes on our next away trip - it's a four day job so perhaps there will be some variety!

Cards on the train for the first time this season. It doesn't work out too well. Bruce Stuckey has joined the "hearts" school and it soon becomes clear he can't play. After three hours of coaching from Gary Peters he still hasn't learned by the time we get to Lincoln.

I've opted for the knock-out whist school but Steve Death can't change THAT pound again, so no-one's getting paid!

Still the boredom is relieved with references to Ray's blazer, my column, and other trivialities.

We don't officially know the team yet. The team sheet had said "from" which, in theory, meant I could be playing but I'm pretty certain it will be an unchanged side.

Naturally I'm less than delighted with that but the lads have done so well, and some very good players are not even in the 12 that I don't mind as much as I might in different circumstances.

I'm a strong possible rather than a probable; certainty, it seems, is as far away as ever.

A probable is a first team member, a possible is a reserve and a certainty is, well, what we all hope to become.

The twelfth man exists in a kind of limbo. He's part of the team yet while they are doing well he will remain a fringe figure. Being part of the team he wants them to do well yet he knows that if they do badly it may mean his recall from the sidelines.

HAVOC

This emotional see-saw can play havoc with one's loyalties - the good guy in you says "All the best lads," the bad guy "For

God's sake lose". Occasionally simple hypocrisy is necessary.

Arriving at Lincoln there's plenty of time to look at the pitch and focus on the opposition.

The pitch is good and Lincoln will be difficult. The presence of Percy Freeman indicates plenty of aerial attacks, the presence of Sam Ellis means that Robin would be well advised to wear his pads back to front!

For the first half the game goes well for us. Lincoln are a good, honest, hard-working side but we have all those qualities and a bit more skill besides. Robin nicks a goal for us and at half-time we're in control.

Often in a game a slight, subconscious shift of attitude can be enough to allow the initiative to slip away from you. That imperceptible change of mood, that unspoken decision to conserve what's been gained and suddenly you find yourself defending out of habit. You develop a siege mentality, invite pressure and inevitably you pay the ultimate penalty.

No matter how good your side, how well prepared you are, such things will happen as they did to us at Lincoln.

In a matter of minutes we've blown it and unlike the Crewe game there is not enough time to fight back.

The atmosphere in our dressing room is strained. Losers' dressing rooms are unpleasant places to be in and that's how it should be. We feel guilty. We had the game won and to toss it away was unforgiveable. Worse, it was unprofessional.

The inquest begins in the bath. "Who crossed the ball?", "Who should have been picking him up?" The questions fly back and forth, the answers conflicting, confused. Emotions are high, rational discussion impossible...

It is the usual human response to defeat, a ritual played out across the land at twenty to five every Saturday afternoon.

At some clubs used to defeat it is meaningless, a gesture, forgotten by five o'clock. For some players the guilt is quickly erased, usually by the second lager.

What's impressive about our team is that the inquest goes on, in the bar, on the station while waiting for the train home and over gammon and chips (and lager) during the journey.

The boss has said little yet. He will have his say on Monday.

MONDAY

Normally our day off, we report to the Adwest training ground subdued. We're all possibles now. As a club we care about a bad result; we will work damn hard this week to get things right. That is the way it is at good clubs.

Every game throws up a problem, defensively, in mid-field, or in attack. The good clubs spend the week working on them; the bad clubs spend Saturdays paying for not working.

The boss goes over Saturday's game with us; the

problems constructively examined, the search not for scapegoats but for solutions. The criticism is fair and is accepted as such.

Later we have a practice game. Changes are made, perhaps more will be before Saturday. Everyone is sharp, it's a good working atmosphere. I am pleased to be a probable again.

TUESDAY

A hard, physical morning. An hour's pressure running in the driving rain.

While we're going through it we moan like hell but afterwards, as we soak gratefully in a hot bath, we feel better. Our guilt is eased by suffering.

WEDNESDAY

A nice change of scenery - training in the secluded countryside at Cold Ash. It's a beautiful autumn morning, sun shining; how lucky we are.

We are having a practice game, with Saturday's team not yet decided. Another chance for possibles to shine.

These games are an invaluable chance to learn more about each other's habits, to develop understanding.

THURSDAY

A day off - most welcome for your columnist who is rapidly falling behind his deadline.

Robin swears that the only reason Ray wears such ridiculous gear is to get a mention.

Steve Death says he never reads it but I'm hopeful that the Sporting Life might print it specially for him.

Stewart Henderson prefixes every conversation with "You won't quote me?" Don't worry Stewart, your secret is safe with me (for the moment).

Ray's efforts for a rival paper have earned him the nickname "Kipling" again from Robin (why is Robin having a go at Ray?)

FRIDAY

Waiting for the team sheet is like sitting in the dentist's waiting room, and there's nothing like a defeat to intensify that feeling.

Possibles are hopeful, probables anxious and certainties smug.

When the sheet goes up everyone casually sprints over to discover their fate. If your name is on it there's nothing to worry about - until tomorrow.

How do you analyse the matches afterwards?

"Did the people pick up the people they were supposed to? Were they looking for possession or hiding? Were there moments of complacency, relaxation, mental laziness or sometimes physical cowardice?"

"Mostly it's mental sloppiness that causes goals and mostly players know it's their fault. You don't want to blame them but make them conscious for next time. If the guy holds his hands up... fair enough, don't do it again. If he won't own up you're fucked, you don't know what he'll do next week."

"The manager's job is to say "Look you did it" and 100% of the time players will admit it because they know the manager knows, but if the manager's weak, he wouldn't always know for one, and he wouldn't always confront the player if he was a strong player."

"It's important the player knows there's someone who sees when he doesn't do his stuff or opts out of his responsibilities, that's the discipline, it makes them less likely to opt out next time. The idea of inquests is that they're signposts of where we're weak. You have got to put some filling in that hole. If the guy's slow you have to compensate for him."

"The dynamic of a football team is a complicated and difficult thing to explain. The key to it is identifying what strengths and weaknesses exist in that collection of players and deploying those strengths. We were organised in that sense. The strength of the side was Robin. We didn't give goals away. As soon as we lost possession we took up our positions, did our thing. We were a footballing side rather than anything else. We would play the ball from the back."

After the defeat at Lincoln only two points separated the top twelve of the division. Stewart Henderson and Steve Hetzke lost their first team places, being replaced by Eamon Dunphy, who from here on in was almost 'a certainty' and Geoff Barker who never quite made it to 'probable' status.

Reading won their next three games, at home against Watford and then twice away in three days - at Workington and Hartlepool.

COCKS OF THE HARSH NORTH

EVENING POST, 27 SEPTEMBER 1975

A marvellous last weekend that began at 9.30am Friday and ended 90 hours later at 5.30am Tuesday.

We'd travelled hundreds of miles from 'wonderful Workington' through 'delightful Darlington' to 'heavenly Hartlepool,' hit the top of the table and had a lot of laughs. But the most important thing was the football, we'd done the business and won the games.

Without that the laughter would have had a hollow ring, the miles would have seemed endless.

A trip like that is a test not so much of a team's skill, but of its character.

The harsh north has often exposed the pretensions of early season high flyers. It was nice therefore to confirm so emphatically that our promotion challenge will not founder north of Watford.

Of the two games the one at Workington was the toughest.

They outplayed us in the first half and if they had finished well would have been a couple of goals ahead at half-time.

Fortunately they suffered the kind of luck that fate seems to reserve for strugglers.

We dominated the second half and with strikers like ours that means the chances were taken for what was eventually a comfortable win.

Nowhere does the gap between the divisions show itself more than in the crucial matter of taking scoring opportunities.

A defensive lapse in the Fourth Division is far less likely to be punished than the same mistake in a higher division.

That is why players like Robin Friday, Jack Whitham, Ray Hiron and John Murray are priceless. Nothing goes begging with these guys around, yet a side like Workington, who in many respects are not so bad, labour in vain with just four goals to their credit before today.

At the end of the game one couldn't help feeling sorry for the Workington players.

For theirs must surely be the toughest job in sport. Bad results, a small yet cynical band of supporters and constant doubt about the future of the club. All of that, plus the thousands of fruitless miles spent journeying in search of elusive glory. Some glory game for them!

By comparison Hartlepool is quite plush!

It's a lot harder, too, to feel sympathy for their players, some of whom fancy themselves as "hard men". Hard in this context is, of course, a euphemism!

Saturday's win, having taken us to the top of the table, gave us, perhaps, a preview of what's in store for us in the months ahead. If that's the case well I think we can safely say we'll manage.

To put it crudely we gave them a right chasing. For Jack Whitham, who played despite a badly bruised foot, it was a personal triumph. His three goals were the climax of a fruitful footballing weekend.

Our trip wasn't all work and although laughs are hard to come by on a wet Friday night we managed to generate our own fun.

Apart from all those silly jokes about Ray's clothes (you should see his new yellow sweater!) the main source of pleasure was the musical talents of the group.

Jack Whitham is an accomplished folk singer with over 160 of his own compositions, Geoff Barker plays the guitar sweetly and Bruce Stuckey plays the guitar!

Jack is great. He enjoys singing and is sensitive enough to do justice to the beautiful contemporary folk lyrics he sings.

Geoff's problem is matching his fine guitar playing with the words which he tends to forget, hence lots of la la las.

Bruce's problem I'm not so sure about. He plays the guitar professionally and rumours that he developed his turn of foot avoiding irate ticket buyers are not true!

Next Wednesday we entertain QPR in a testimonial game for Jim Wallbanks, who has been a great servant to the club.

Player, manager, coach and now physio, Jimmy has spent a lifetime in football. He richly deserves this occasion and it promises to be a great night for him and for anyone who can get to Elm Park. If you can be there, come.

If you love your football you must come to Rangers. They are unquestionably the most exciting English team of recent years. They have what so much of our football has lacked in recent years - style.

Not since the Spurs "double" side of the early 60's have we seen a team committed to developing its skill to the highest possible level, refusing to sacrifice its most skilful players to methods of lesser mortals.

In effect what Rangers are saying is this - it is possible to win the First Division without "ball winners" who can't play, strong men who can run through mud, but can't pass the ball accurately and without intimidating your opponents.

In our modern game that is quite a bold statement to make. Many of our recently successful sides seemed to regard football as a form of all-in wrestling.

Rangers, and others, notably Derby, West Ham and Manchester United, see it more as a game of chess.

With players such as Bowles, Francis, Givens, Thomas, Masson and Parkes they are well equipped to succeed this season. If they do, English football will regain much of its self-respect and lose the unwanted worldwide tag of "Oh yes ze English - zey very strong" - as a Spaniard on holiday put it to me.

So if you can get to Elm Park on Wednesday bring your son and your wife. It might prove to them that football can be a delight when played in the right spirit.

Who knows, you might even get the flavour and start watching us.

QPR finished runners-up to Liverpool the following May and slaughtered Reading that night scoring three in quarter of an hour and easing up considerably.

"I remember a lot of trips to the North of England that season. Robin and the other southern lads called it khazi country. I liked the challenge of being on the road."

Jack Whitham, who once scored a hat-trick for Liverpool in front of the Kop, started and finished his goalscoring record at Reading with those three at Hartlepool. He never scored another league goal much to our amazement. Compared with Ray Hiron he looked the business but was never quite there.

Some games are much, much more significant than others even though the same number of points is at stake. Good results are both foundation stones and yardsticks. The draw at Crewe had shown the side's spirit, the defeat at Lincoln its limitations and now the game against Bournemouth its promotion-winning potential. The first part of the season turned on the match in which Reading showed their staying power in front of the TV cameras and a large crowd of 7,226. They were top and hadn't conceded a goal at home.

I remember it well as an exciting and nasty match, the kind that gives you a sick feeling if you don't win and a real clenched fist buzz if you do. One nil down with Robin Friday already in the bath, sent off for fighting Stuart Morgan, an ex-Reading player, and the Bournemouth hordes braying, (they're not at all as genteel as their town), Reading were in trouble throwing it away again, we thought. To my mind this became Dunphy's match, his singular, most obvious contribution to Reading. He took control of the mid-field and scored two superb late goals from the edge of the box. Now, it clearly had less of an impact on Eamon's memory. He vaguely recalls it as scoring two goals in a 3-2 win over Stockport!

EAMON'S BRACE PICKS OFF CHERRIES

EVENING POST, 4 OCTOBER 1975

"In politics a week is a long time" - wise words from that wily old pragmatist Harold WIlson.

He might just as well have been talking about football where life is equally uncertain and memories stretch little further than the last game.

This week's two-goal "hero" very often becomes next week's no-goal bum, the cheers very quickly turn to jeers.

It's a part of the game you learn with experience to accept, it doesn't pay to fly too high when things are going well or, for that matter, to get suicidal when times are hard.

Such thoughts are prominent in my head after last Saturday's game and while they didn't detract from the pleasure of scoring two goals - they helped to put things in perspective.

MOODS

For first hand evidence of the game's changing moods one had to look no further than Jack Whitham - Monday's hat-trick hero, substituted five days later.

As it is for individuals, so it is for teams - complacency is a luxury you can ill-afford whether you're a goal scoring "hero" or a promotion chasing team.

Players, like teams, should be judged in terms of months rather than weeks. With seven months and 38 games of the season left, a great many pit-falls to be faced and overcome, our credentials for heroism will often be tested. If we win promotion next April then, perhaps, we can take our bow.

Last Saturday's game presented us with a problem that will frequently be with us this season. Bournemouth came to Elm Park to play it tight, putting plenty of bodies between ball and goal in the hope of "nicking" a point. For a while it seemed as if they might get both points and no doubt they would have, had our recent success softened us up.

SERIOUS

The situation was serious when with 20 minutes to go we found ourselves 1-0 down and in many ways those final minutes were the most significant of the season so far.

A question had been asked of our character to which we could have replied in a number of ways. Losing is always bad but to lose at home, when top of the "table", in front of the best crowd of the year, is humiliating.

So at 4.20 last Saturday another factor loomed large in our minds - fear. The fear of losing is always a potent force in the game and nowhere is that element more destructive than when it takes hold of players in front of their own fans.

Away from home it drives men on the fuel with which to run themselves aimlessly into the ground, the "Dutch courage" with which to embark on suicidal tackles.

Playing at home the problems and the solutions are different. Before your own fans who, if things aren't going well, will be having a moan, the fear is not only of losing but of making a fool of yourself. It's an individual as well as collective anxiety. At home you've got to get on the ball, got to try to create something and while fear can make you run faster or tackle harder it can't help you to pass accurately, or shoot straighter.

Confronted with that kind of situation last Saturday, as no doubt we will in the future, we reacted as a good side should.

We kept playing good football, everyone looking for the ball, there was no panic, no recriminations and, in the end, no disaster.

Under those circumstances victory is indeed sweet because it tells you more about the depth of character within the side, than a more easily gained success.

It also indicates that we can remain a team through a bad patch and not disintegrate to a rabble at the first sign of defeat, a common and depressing feature of many "successful" sides.

The idea that "we are all in it together" may, in the often cynical world of professional sport, be something of a myth. But it is a piece of mythology that it is essential to preserve in a promotion-chasing team.

The "we" in this instance means not only the eleven players involved in a particular game but, and I make no apology for repeating this, everyone at the club and most importantly those who support us. In this respect the crowd reaction to last Saturday's "crisis" was really encouraging.

It is, I believe, an indisputable fact that good supporters can play a crucial role in helping a club to achieve success.

Assuming that out of 20 odd home games at least half a dozen will be tight, in-the-balance affairs, it follows that the "lift" players get from a sympathetic crowd will tip the scales in favour of the home team.

The six points subsequently gained is a massive contribution to promotion and proof, if such were needed, that a good club-supporter relationship is not merely a matter of PR.

I would mark the two points we gained last week down to our supporters.

Recognising that while such a game is difficult to play in, it can't for the first hour, have been much fun to watch either.

Last week Freddie Goodwin, this week Gerry Summers

and Steve Burtenshaw. Next week - who knows?

October is a dangerous month for football managers and it is safe to predict that within the next few weeks the nation's already lengthy dole queues will be joined by more of this hardy breed.

At this time of year, when summer's dream turns to autumn nightmare, the search for a scapegoat begins and invariably the trail leads to the manager's office.

It's a depressing business. The pointed Press speculation, the loaded questions, the shifty glances, leading inevitably in an atmosphere of rapidly diminishing morale, to the final bitter act.

FAILURE
As players we often forget the harsh realities of the manager's job and the final distressing consequences of his failure.

We get the "needle" when we're dropped or given less than our due. We forget that we are several steps further from the dole queue than he is.

For us there is always another club, the chance to start afresh, for out-of-work managers the job opportunities are on a par with those of street lamp lighters.

The reasons for their failures are many. Too little time in which to develop a young side, too little money to attract badly-needed players, or simply failure to meet the demands of a job that calls for so many qualities.

Given the nature of our game, such hiring and firing is inevitable. Few have any illusions about the job before they take it on.

Whether they succeed or fail these brave men and their families deserve our admiration, and, in their passing, our sympathy.

"It was a good win", recalls Eamon. A side that knows it can come from behind to get a result, and has recent experience of it, is always more dangerous. Having come back at Crewe and beaten Bournemouth, Reading were 'psychologically' well-prepared.

It prompted Eamon to consider the wider value of his own experience to Reading.

"I brought to Reading from a very good Millwall side a set of basic notions or ideas about the game that were very pure and very firm. There was no fucking about, everyone did their job when we had the ball and when we didn't and if they didn't there was a row. You have to have people who know what's right and wrong in football terms and impose it on the others."

"I was doing a job for Charlie in the dressing room. There were a few rogues in there - Fourth Division footballers by virtue of the fact they're in the Fourth Division usually have something wrong with them."

"I didn't have to come to Reading. It was a come-down to play there, so I was going to make it worthwhile. It was a question of imposing those attitudes on a club that hadn't had them. Charlie Hurley's failure as a manager was that he wasn't able to impose those disciplines from the position he held and consequently it remained a mystery to Charlie why we were succeeding."

"It was this failure on his part to understand how the team was succeeding that unfortunately led to his demise. He actually thought it was him that was responsible for the success."

At this stage in the season, (the fourth home win and top of the table), the crowd were still with the team, though in this particular game antagonism towards Stuart Morgan, would have contributed to their vocal support.

"A hostile, cynical crowd would have got at us that day", thought Eamon.

"The humour of the supporters makes a great deal of difference and that humour is formed by past experiences, expectations and many other things. The humour of a crowd does affect the players and sometimes affects them very badly. The humour of the crowd away from home doesn't matter, however hostile they are, it doesn't matter. The home crowd is a great indispensable ally to have."

"How did you feel about the crowd at Reading?" I asked.

"Remember I came from Millwall where the crowd was very special, a unique atmosphere there. I thought the crowd at Reading were OK. In a way they reflected the town, they weren't very anything. They were OK. We gave them a good year that year. Next year I can't remember them being very bad. I remember them being quiet. At Millwall they'd be either one thing or the other."

It's a fair judgement on the Elm Park faithful. Unlike most 'Kops', the South Bank is along the side of the pitch rather than behind the goal. Together with a history of under-achievement and the low-key nature of football within the town, it means we've always seemed a pretty docile lot. We only sing when absolutely necessary. But we care just as much.

Though Reading had won that day the crowd's doubts were to creep back over the next few results. The following week they were unable to pull back a two goal deficit at lowly Scunthorpe. An unchanged team beat Bradford City at Elm Park and then travelled to Barnsley. Eamon Dunphy takes up the case.

ON TRIAL AT BARNSLEY

EVENING POST, 25 OCTOBER 1975

DATE: Sunday, October 19.

CASE: People v Dunphy.

CHARGES: Misleading the Public.

Defendant made loud claims on behalf of Reading FC, thereby causing the public to believe the aforementioned football club would win promotion this season.

PUBLIC PROSECUTOR: How does the defendant plead - guilty or not guilty?

DEFENDANT: Not guilty.

PP: You lost 4-2 at Barnsley yesterday. Doesn't that suggest that promotion is no more than a figment of your imagination?

D: Nonsense, sure it was a shock but even the best sides get hammered occasionally.

PP: At Barnsley?

D: Well, Leeds once lost 7-0 at West Ham.

PP: You're suggesting that you're in the same class as Leeds are you?

D: No, I'm just trying to point out that football can be a funny game.

PP: Spare us the cliches, next you will be telling us that you played well.

D: It's funny you should say that. As a matter of fact we did play quite well.

PP: Now that's funny! You lost 4-2 and played well.

D: I would qualify that. We played well going forward. We scored two goals and created four or five good chances; that's not bad away from home. We played the better football; in fact, the Barnsley supporters said we were the best side they've seen this season.

PP: Were they sober?

D: Just.

PP: You're taking all this a bit light-heartedly, aren't you? It's a serious business, you know.

D: You don't have to tell me that, it's my living. Nobody likes losing but it doesn't help to start screaming every time it happens. The season is 46 games long; we will lose again before next April, maybe even at home; there's no need to panic. The important thing is to stick to your beliefs and to learn from your defeats; moaning doesn't help. Obviously we're not happy about Saturday, but we're a good side, we've got a good manager, we'll sort things out by Monday night.

PP: What did you learn from the defeat at Barnsley?

D: That it's not good enough to be a good side going forward, that it's equally important, particularly away from home, to defend well.

PP: Are you saying your defence let you down? Let's face it, four goals conceded it looks bad for them, doesn't it?

D: Them? There's no Us and Them in football; there's just one unit. We attack together, defend together. It doesn't follow that because we conceded four goals our defenders had a "nightmare". What it means is that we defended badly as a side.

PPP: I'm not sure I follow that. Are you saying that if the ball is knocked into your penalty area and a goal is scored that that is the forwards' fault?

D: More or less. Look at it this way. My job as a midfield player is to create scoring chances when we're in possession and to stop the opposition midfield players doing so when they've got the ball. If they create a lot of chances in our area and we give goals away under pressure, I may well be the cause of the problem. If forwards don't defend well it can make defenders' jobs impossible.

PP: So that's what happened at Barnsley?

D: It was an important factor.

PP: If you knew all this beforehand why didn't you do something about it?

D: I suppose you think that's clever?

PP: You're here to answer questions, get on with it.

D: OK, I'll try to explain. Football is a game of moods. If you're going well, you feel confident, you're afraid of no-one. You're hungry for the ball, you want to attack, everything flows, the chances go in. All your opponents' chances hit the post. Although the game is never easy you're on top of it. You've no fear, no anxiety. That's the way it's been for us for most of the season. We've outplayed every side we've met including Third Division Gillingham. Every time we've played we've expected to win. Of course, you can't go through a season like that. Something always happens - Barnsley was our "something". We weren't afraid of them, yet fear is an important element in football. Fear is a good motivator, particularly when it comes to defending. We've been enjoying the game so much going forward, that we've tended to relax when the opposition have the ball. Saturday taught us not to relax.

PP: It's an interesting theory, what does it mean?

D: It means that when we go to Newport on Monday we will be more aware of our defensive duties. It's just a slight shift of emphasis.

PP: I suppose that means a boring 0-0 draw.

D: It might be boring for you but I think we could live with it.

PP: Haven't you got a duty to entertain?

D: We did at Barnsley. Football is sometimes a matter of priorities and ours is promotion.

PP: You're still confident then?

D: Yes. We were a good side before Saturday and we're still a good side. It would take more than one defeat to shake our confidence. You know sometimes I get the feeling that people are waiting for some dramatic collapse, expecting us to suddenly slide down the "table".

PP: It's happened before.

D: Well, it won't happen this season.

PP: We'll see.

D: At Newport, I hope.

PP: I believe you get a "fat bonus" if you get a point at Newport to put you in the top four after 12 games.

D: Correct.

PP: A new car, perhaps?

D: It's not that "fat", perhaps a new suit! Or perhaps some thing off my overdraft.

PP: Overdraft?

D: You'd be surprised.

PP: Has Ray Hiron got one?

D: No. Ray's lucky, he's got his pension so he's quite well off. He's buying five suits with his bonus.

PP: Five suits?

D: Yes. He gets his for £7.50 you know. Nice tailor on the Isle of Wight.

PP: Why don't you leave Ray alone?

D: Who, me?

NB. to Sports Editor. If we lose at Newport I'm leaving the country. Forward the cheque to Swiss Bank.

Two days later, with young defenders Gary Peters and Bobby Lenarduzzi dropped and John 'the luxury item' Murray rested, Reading ground out the aforesaid 0-0 draw at Newport County.

Hurley may have picked the team and gone for the experience of Henderson, Youlden and Whitham but with just a quarter of the season gone Dunphy is quite clear in his own mind about how the team was being run.

"Reading should never have been in the Fourth Division with the resources at Charlie's disposal and the players he had there when I arrived. He only needed a bit of character in the dressing room. The players were a mixture of the wayward and the timid - Youlden, Moreline, Henderson - they were big imposing defenders but very timid lads. They hated what Robin Friday and Minty did, they hated all that stuff but they thought what the fuck can we do about it."

"They wouldn't have got promotion if Gordon Cumming and myself hadn't been there. We were the two key people in terms of leadership and in terms of performance. The crowd used to get on to us a lot. The whole thing would have crumbled in terms of leadership if we'd not been there."

"Charlie just used to say 'come on' and that shite. He knew nothing, we did it for him, that's the job I did for him, get them organised on the pitch, get the dressing room spirit up."

As an ordinary terrace fan you don't, of course, see or hear any of this. You just might get to sense it on the pitch if you've got good, sensitive, experienced antennae. But, at the time, I took Hurley's programme notes - and Dunphy's columns which express respect for the manager - at face value!

The Barnsley defeat seemed to take a heavy toll on the team's morale. Perhaps because the leaders had kept on winning...

		Played	Points
1.	Lincoln	14	22
2.	Northampton	14	22
3.	Tranmere	14	20
4.	Reading	14	19
5.	Doncaster	14	18
6.	Bournemouth	14	17

...or perhaps it was just the change of season as the tail of a long, hot summer faded away. The football seemed to get grittier and more desperate from here on in. Or perhaps it was just the looming shadow of the dour Huddersfield Town, who visited Elm Park on 25 October.

THE DEAD MARCH

EVENING POST, 1 NOVEMBER 1975

As Evening Post readers will have gathered the talking point in the dressing room after last Saturday's game was the amazing reaction of a section of our supporters to the afternoon's sport.

Most of what was said is unprintable and would have made even Richard Nixon blush.

Indeed when David Dibben solicited an after-match comment from your normally cool, rational columnist, the reply was short, sharp and four lettered.

When I joined the club I was warned about the "notorious section of the fans", a warning I chose to disregard in the belief that by and large a club gets the support it deserves.

I still believe that to be true, but I must admit last Saturday's events cause me to have second thoughts. In the 15 years I've been a "pro" I've never heard a successful team subjected to the kind of abuse we heard last Saturday. You don't expect the "Dead March" when you're in the top four!

The game was a difficult one for Huddersfield had not lost away from home this season, had only conceded three goals and are themselves challenging for promotion.

They've also got a few "heavies" who are not averse to putting some "stick" about. They defend well because they don't allow you to play football. They deny you space to work the ball, aiming all the time to stop flowing movement of the kind that our crowd is used to seeing.

As the away side they did a good job. Success away from home means frustrating the home team and, equally important, the home crowd.

MURMURS

If the crowd start "getting" at the home players you can be sure life will be a lot easier for the away team. The home players, reluctant to become the focus of the crowd's frustration, will either start to hide or get rid of the ball as quickly as possible in the general direction of their opponent's goal.

That in a nutshell is what Huddersfield tried to achieve. In doing so they were well within their rights. We shall be doing the same at Doncaster this afternoon, although I hope with more class and less cynicism.

The best way to overcome these tactics is to be patient, continue to try to play football, not resort to thumping the ball great distances and, above all, not be intimidated by your own crowd.

That, to our credit, is what we tried to do last Saturday.

It was difficult at times, for it's not only supporters who feel the urge to "kick and rush". But if you're a "pro" your head must rule your heart.

After 15 minutes I could hear the murmurs from the crowd. "Get on with it", a loud moan when Tommy Youlden, quite correctly, pushed a long ball to Steve Death, impatience spreading, grist to the Huddersfield mill.

At this point both the moaners in the crowd and our opponents are hoping for the same thing - they both want us to abandon our beliefs and to mount an aerial attack on their penalty area. Our attacks would become predictable, their defence would never be drawn, our supporters would get sore throats, their defenders sore heads, net result 0-0 draw.

Lots of action, no danger. I wonder how often this season Huddersfield's opponents have resorted to such tactics?

We didn't and in the end we got our reward - how fitting that Gordon Cumming should score the decisive goal. For "Riddle", abuse from the home crowd has become a way of life, yet this inscrutable little man has as much guts and professionalism as any player I've seen.

To have survived the vicious abuse he's taken from our "supporters" over the years calls for a degree of moral courage that is probably beyond the comprehension of his critics.

What provokes such unbelievable behaviour? As it surely can't be the present position of the club the answer must lie in the past history of the club, in the frustration of those whose hopes have been repeatedly dashed, who have seen too many false dawns and who wait expectantly for us to plunge down the table as so often before.

For them every defeat heralds the "big slide", every anxious moment of a game spells imminent disaster.

Last Saturday's game was full of anxious moments. At times it seemed, even to us, that a draw was the most we'd get. In my view the abuse that came our way is the legacy of years of frustration and out of all proportion to the happenings of one game.

SUPPORT

To those who doubt, and who can blame them, I say this. The team we have at present started this season with a clean slate. We've done well. We neither know nor care about the past. I can assure you of this. If there ever was some "special disease" that afflicted this club before it no longer exists. We've got one hell of a chance of promotion this season, but to get there we need genuine support.

Supporting your team does not mean becoming an uncritical zombie. But go to Anfield, Goodison, Old Trafford, Millwall or Lincoln City and you will find a commitment that is worth ten points a season to their team.

When we played Lincoln recently we took a one goal lead to which their crowd reacted by cheering even louder. The players responded and Lincoln won the game and consequently now have a two point lead over us. Their support was a major factor in that victory.

APPRECIATED

From the letters that have arrived at the club this week and those published in the Evening Post it is clear that many of our loyal fans have been upset by the cynicism of the minority. They can rest assured that their support is appreciated in the dressing room. When we win promotion it will be a very real pleasure to have done so for them.

As for the others - well, you can be sure of one thing, the "fans" who are crying the loudest now will be shouting the loudest when we do go "up" and I bet they won't even feel guilty! That's life.

Well, to put the boot on the other foot for a change, aren't players fickle? Only a month ago Eamon was praising the Reading crowd's contribution to the victory over Bournemouth.

Neither of us would have actually remembered this incident without prompting. In itself it was a storm in a tea-cup but it also acts as a vivid insight into the paradoxical nature of the player's relationship with his team's supporters; accepting their praise but denying their opportunity to criticise.

Fifty or a hundred blokes, probably drunk, humming 'The Dead March' for a few minutes during a dull passage of a dull game on a dull afternoon. As football 'chants' go it might even be considered sophisticated and amusing nowadays.

(The following season, with Reading deep in relegation trouble, an unusually graphic and prescient Hurley wrote in his programme notes, "I can see the vultures gathering on the roof of the stand." As the opposition's second goal went in the South Bank burst into a chorus of "Bring on the vultures").

Eamon, however, in this column translated a general and lightweight criticism of the team into the need for a specific and full-blooded defence of a particular player. He goes on to describe the mentality of the 'knockers'.

"I don't remember the incident, but I do remember Gordon Cumming was always taking stick because they didn't know his value as a player. The way they measure value is usually in spectaculars and he wasn't spectacular. I was the same kind of player in many ways. Crowds used to take a quick look at you and take an instant dislike to you, the way you look. It didn't scare me, I was tough enough inside."

"There is a certain type of person who goes on a football terrace, not really sensitive to what's happening at all on the pitch. There's an element in all football crowds, who are really just there to jeer and have no feelings for the game. For guys like that, disastrous matches or failure like that is a kind of therapy in a kind of weird way. It's all understandable in psychological terms, in primitive, animal terms."

"What's going on in football matches is a ritual. The behaviour of people at football matches reflects the sort of society you have. However, in a footballer's boots you feel the violence of it and the torment and pressure of it and you must understand, as footballers don't understand when they're playing or even afterwards, what we are and why we're there and what function we're performing for society in a cultural sense."

"In Cumming's case they started digging in at him, (and I think they even started having a go at me at some stage), and he then needed defending. He was a very valuable player who wasn't perceived to be a valuable player. He'd been part of the club for a while and people had ideas about him one way or the other. The longer you're at a club the more people have an idea about you and the idea they had about him was wrong and so he was the butt of an element of the crowd."

Trying to remember just what was and wasn't Gordon Cumming's contribution that season is probably beyond anyone now. But it's clear from the feelings expressed here that 'knocking' has an effect. For players to claim "It doesn't affect me at all" is clearly nonsense.

There are two kinds of knocking - that which comes from a few unbalanced, embittered individuals in the crowd (which should be easily overcome) and that from hundreds or thousands of fans jeering or booing in unison.

The player's response to both is identical; grow a thick skin and don't take criticism from anyone outside the game. The public on-the-field resilience of professional footballers, who are also sometimes young and volatile people, in the face of terrible and harsh abuse, is absolutely admirable but off the field, in their private lives, they make the whole crowd pay a price by excluding them.

In 'The Dead March' column Eamon says supporting does not mean being an 'uncritical zombie'. Quite right, too; going to football is both spectating and participating. The crowd collectively expresses encouragement, appreciation, criticism and derision. They are capable of examining the team's performance as a whole and also that of individuals within it. They can attempt to 'make' the appropriate substitutions.

When five thousand, or twenty five thousand, experienced football-watchers come to a collective verdict on what's happening on the pitch are their views of no worth at all to the experts?

In one sense the fan has a very pure perspective. He or she is able to judge the player solely under match conditions - not at all influenced by their performances on the training ground or the agenda in the manager's mind. What the fan sees is what the club ultimately gets - real points not training ground plaudits.

I have, I freely confess, on occasion booed and jeered Reading players who, in my view and that of many others, have not been performing in the best interests of the club. Sometimes they have been removed. In one notable recent instance the tactics have been drastically changed, the victim looks good again and I cheer him once more. I do not feel two-faced about this. I feel that, collectively, we, the crowd, have made constructive criticism.

Eamon rightly recognises different types of supporter, including our old enemy 'the mindless moron' and also the loyal followers. He doesn't however, recognise the constructively critical role. Unfortunately the crowd is unable to chant: "Get someone with pace to fill in alongside the ageing centre half" with one voice so what they do cry tends to sound like personal abuse.

There is certain to be conflict where the objectives and priorities of different groups clash. For the supporter (and the club), the players are means to an end. The players' relationship with the club is more intense, knowledgeable and productive but essentially short-lived. In the column Eamon says that the players "neither know nor care about the past" which is a terrible thing for the supporter of the club to hear. His identity as a fan is bound up in it. Yet the player sees it from a different, but to him, equally vital perspective.

"The fan can walk from the club at the end of the match. He goes there for recreation. For us it was life itself. Some supporters have a different kind of loyalty but for the vast majority of supporters it's a bit of recreation, a chance to vent a bit of spleen, get it off your chest, see something exciting."

"I'm not slagging supporters off but I'm saying they don't quite understand how much a lot of guys give, how much of themselves they invest. Geoff Barker's wife, why was she in Reading at all except that he could serve the club at £50 per week at a time when the minimum wage in industry was at least that, and job prospects much better and pensions and all that went with it. There were no pensions in football, no superannuation in football."

"Fans are important but you're not actually doing if for them. You're doing it for yourself. You know the ultimate truth is if you break your leg you go to hospital but the fans go home for tea. It's your job that's lost not theirs."

Maybe, but I know a few people who spend a large dollop of their wages supporting the club for whom it's a lot more than 'a bit of recreation'. In the end, as Eamon acknowledges later, it is their club; unlike the player, they can't get another one.

Victory over challenging Huddersfield, then, tinged with some bitterness in the dressing room. A very useful draw was obtained at Doncaster followed by two home wins, 1-0 over Swansea and 4-3 over Exeter. Reading remained in fourth place three points behind leaders Northampton.

THAT MAN FRIDAY

EVENING POST, 15 NOVEMBER 1975

Last Saturday's dramatic win over Exeter was the week's good news but the bad news came on Tuesday when we learned of Robin Friday's three match suspension.

The big man will be badly missed particularly as the games will be away from home unless we draw at Hendon, in which case the replay will be Robin's last game off.

Robin Friday is unique. It is difficult to measure his influence on our side, for one has to take into account not only his talent as a player but the sheer power of his presence which invariably intimidates our opponents, and is a source of inspiration to us lesser mortals who play with him.

Against Exeter last Saturday he gave a typically brave and powerful performance, yet before the game he was visibly weakened by flu and probably should not have played. It was our good fortune that he did, for it was primarily his skill and aggression that won for us a game that could so easily have been lost.

ALWAYS

On his day, and that's nearly always, Robin is unflappable, a defender's nightmare, not merely power and aggression, but delicate skill and vision.

For most defenders the task is too much and long before the end they are reduced to nervous wrecks. Goalkeepers cower on their line, hapless centre backs challenge without conviction and we pick up the goals.

Some, the braver ones, resort to violence. I have never seen a player take as much unfair punishment so often as Robin does. It never stops him but, naturally, it leads to him retaliating, an act which refs, who somehow miss the original foul, are never slow to spot.

This season I've seen whole defences line up to take turns at kicking Robin. None have been sent off; most escaped with a severe dose of finger-wagging (which is quite painless).

Robin is good enough to play at any level of the game. He would be just as potent a force in the First Division, a thought which prompts the question - what is he doing in the Fourth Division?

WELCOME

The answer lies in the wild, extravagant nature of the man and the prejudices of many leading managers whose ideal player is a lion on the field and a lamb off it.

Robin Friday, the player, would be welcome at any club.
Robin Friday, the citizen, would cause many to cringe.

Robin is a non-conformist. Scruffy jeans, long hair, likes a drink, never runs away from aggro, doesn't keep curate's hours or use curate's language. No, he doesn't conform, not in any way.

Unlike most hard men there is no badness in him. He wouldn't go "over the top" to another player. He wouldn't shirk a hard training session the morning after the night before.

He is a generous friend, first to buy a drink or to offer his last pound to a mate. Charming company after a game, reassuring in those nervous minutes before the off, a good soldier in the battle.

No side, no fear, nothing sly, a magnet for all that's good, and bad, in life.

That he should be in the Fourth Division says something about our game and the men who decry the lack of talent and originality in it.

TESTIMONY

Robin's success bears testimony to Charlie Hurley's skill and judgement as a manager. It is, too, a superb piece of man management that protects Robin from the excesses of his own wild spirit. That spirit will be badly missed in the next three games.

Nagging injuries have plagued me for the last few weeks. I have spent more time in the treatment room that on the training ground and earned the nickname Aladdin from the lads.

Tommy Youlden has been particularly vocal in his criticism which is not surprising as he is a health and fitness freak and views all injury as a sign of weak spirit.

Rosy-cheeked, full of energy, Tom bursting with health is a bloody nuisance on a cold morning. Nothing worse when you're pale, shrivelled and aching than the sight and sound of "Bionic Man". Do me a favour Tom - keep out of the sick room!

The arrival of the cold weather means renewed acquaintance with old war wounds. The training ground, so idyllic in summer, quickly loses its attraction as the cold winter winds whistle up your track suit bottom. From now on physio Jimmy Wallbanks will become very popular as players take refuge under the warm lamps and the comfort from Jim's soft hands.

Of course it's very unusual to find your columnist in there but I'm really injured (honest).

TYPICAL

Your typical malingerer is a past master at "lying doggo" in the treatment room. He usually appears at this time of year and for him the perfect week's itinerary reads as follows:

MONDAY - Report physio 10am. Strained groin - no

visible evidence, must be deep-seated. 11am. After one hour's heat treatment brave attempt to run. 11.05. It's no good. Feels sore. Physio's advice. Have a hot bath and rest until tomorrow.

TUESDAY - 10am. More heat treatment. 11.00. 15 minutes' running on track. Still feeling it. Hot bath. More rest.

WEDNESDAY - Some reaction to yesterday's running. "Better take it easy," says physio. One hour's heat. Hot bath. More rest.

THURSDAY - Feeling a lot better today. Looks right for Saturday. One hour's heat. Half an hour's running (gentle). More rest.

FRIDAY - The moment of truth. Will he pass fitness test? It feels good. The rest and the heat has worked wonders. A little more heat before test. 11am. Passes fitness test easily, making a few faces for effect. Thinks: "God, it's cold out here." More heat. Hot bath. Another week over.

Memory may play tricks with the facts, the causes, the chronology and our opinions but it preserves, even gilds, the impression of personalities. Neither Eamon nor I could remember Robin without smiling and shaking our heads about Reading FC's favourite villain.

Fifteen years on, that column sounds like strong stuff, especially from one team mate about another. But Eamon couldn't have written it any other way and retained his credibility. Two days after that column Robin was in court in Newport charged with using obscene language. Two months before it, to quote the Evening Post, "Friday's... face looked as though it had been trampled on by a rugby scrum - and that was before the game!" Friday's explanation: "My missus threw a can of beans at me." Really? Which one?

Friday's was a short but brilliant career. For those who never saw him the nearest playing (and physical) analogy might be Mario Kempes the Argentinian World Cup winner of 1978. Tall, long hair, powerful, good dribbler, great shot. But the temperament was something else - an amalgam maybe of early Mike Tyson and late George Best.

He came to the professional game late, joining Reading at 21. He'd been in a bit of trouble and then worked as an asphalter. He played for Hayes against Reading in the FA Cup, did well over the two games and Charlie Hurley signed him a year later as an amateur. He made his debut in a Sunday morning game at Northampton in January 1974.

He was an inspiration, a throwback to the carefree dribbling skills of the nineteenth century. 3-3. He didn't score, but he got four in the next four games. Reading then scored as many in his first five games as they had in the previous nineteen.

A star had emerged and, in time, Friday took his place alongside Blackman, Terry, Chappell, Freeman, Dixon and Senior in the pantheon of great Reading centre-forwards.

It was to Charlie Hurley's great credit that he was both signed and effectively managed. In all he played 121 games for Reading, scoring 46 goals, and in both his full seasons was voted 'Player of the Year'. After falling out with the club he joined Second Division Cardiff City in December 1976 for a mere £30,000. The dour Jimmy Andrews couldn't get the best out of him, he was too far from his native London and after a few games of brilliance, walked out of Ninian Park and League football.

Robin Friday's extravagances and escapades continued to be reported off the sporting pages. Over Christmas 1990, during the writing of this book, came the sad news that he had been found dead in his London flat, at the age of 38.

"We played him to his limits that season", recalls Eamon. "We got him involved in our success and kept him on the rails as far as possible."

"In a way he was a baby. He loved simple basic pleasures. He wouldn't say no to anything. He loved women and women loved him. He was a free spirit. He didn't have the disciplines necessary for professional sport. We got the most out of him anyone could that season. He was not a natural athlete. He had bow-legs, asthma and no pace but he was very brave and powerful. Up north they tried to nail him but he'd never shirk. He was a lovely man socially, very vivacious. I was very pally with him."

Life many not have been kind to Robin, nor he to it but, for what it's worth, he won the battle for first place in our memories.

Following a 0-0 at Torquay, Reading - without Robin Friday (suspended) and Eamon Dunphy (calf injury) - were beaten in the FA Cup First Round by Hendon. It was a humiliating defeat against poor opposition. Jack Whitham never had another proper run in the team. We wondered in the coach on the way home about that old chestnut of "concentrating on the League", otherwise known as the willingness to throw the Cup towel in. The match suggested that without Friday we wouldn't get very far in the promotion race. Eamon devoted his column the following week to a light-hearted quiz about the media personalities in the game.

Victory the following week at Darlington restored his gritty realism.

THIS IS NOT A TIME FOR DOUBT

EVENING POST, 6 DECEMBER 1975

Winning is always good... winning away from home is beautiful.

To say that is what "it's all about" may seem narrow but for us it really is so.

To win is to justify your existence, to pay the price for all that is good in our life - the carefree days spent training, the timeless hours of travel, the glorious schoolboyish irresponsibility of it all.

All those good things are so much richer when the results are right.

Who could fancy a weekend in Darlington? Who would believe it was such fun?

A long coach journey, the hours slipping by broken only by the stops for meals at anonymous eating houses, the odd eruption in the card school (usually involving Gary and Ray) the call for hush as Steve Death strains to catch the racing results on the radio.

It's nice to be away from routine, different food, a nice hotel, a timeless quality - noon, evening, it doesn't matter, a curious sense of freedom.

Listening to the talk. Always on football journeys interesting people, rich humour, good stories.

A break from the card school, listening to the boss. It's "All Our Yesterdays" as he recalls his days at Sunderland. He's talking about Brian Clough, it's interesting, witty and gets better at every telling!

And Minty Murray laconic (I'll tell you what that means on Monday Minty) biting humour zoning in on his targets (Ray, Me, Gary, Tom). Minty sharp... old pro.

David Dibben in his nice new suit. Crossword man (The Sun). Enjoying the company, a part of it all, and yet should we lose tomorrow he would have to say harsh things.

Gary Peters, buttons undone to the navel (our pin-up boy) throwing himself eagerly into the card game. Bursting to play his first game up front. Appetite, that's Gary, wants to play. Somehow comforting to see him so geed up. He'll make things happen tomorrow.

Tomorrow, a job of work to be done. Forget the easy relaxed life style, the nice affectionate feelings. You've got to earn your corn in a tough no-quarter-given game, the tension grips your gut, a mixture of fear and excitement - this is the reality of our lives, and other side of the coin.

A chill in your spine - perhaps we'll blow it today?

CONQUER

No chance. We're a good side now, difficult to beat, sure of ourselves, confident, secure in the knowledge that the fear won't get to us. We know we can conquer it, gee each other up, go out and do the business.

We did.

Many good performances. Firstly, as a unit, that is most important. It simply means having people available when you've got the ball, never being isolated, no lone rangers.

When they've got it, working together to get it back, one man pressurising, the next picking up the pieces. Always having cover, people not simply doing their own jobs but doing yours too if you're caught out.

Deathie marvellously safe, reassuring, Tommy and Geoff winning it in the air; Dave efficient as a computer; Bob constructive; Riddle responsible, probing; Bruce working, Gary a triumph of industry, Minty as sharp in front of goal as in conversation; Ray elegance, class; - Me? Taking notes!

A good side. A promotion side. Now you feel a pride when we run on the field. Pleasure when their crowd purr in appreciation.

Then it's over, you've won. Tired, elated, you soak in the bath. You talk about the chances missed, the narrow escapes, the ref, the kicking, the insults exchanged and wonder how did Lincoln do? Tranmere? Northampton? Doncaster?

Hell, it doesn't matter. We'll do it ourselves.

FOOLISH

This is not a time for doubt. Always before the game you doubt - always . In victory how foolish those doubts seem.

Contentment, the glow of victory settled on in time for a drink, to savour the feeling, bright-eyed, triumphant.

Another week over, another step nearer promotion. Twenty eight games, a lot of battling to go, but it looks very good. Every reason to suppose our dreams will come true.

As I travel down by train each day my mind begins to wander to this fantasy. I go forward to the last game of the season. Elm Park is bursting at the seams, we're in the final minute of the game, we're coasting to a comfortable win.

The final whistle blows, the crowd erupts, laps of honour, much back slapping, the champagne corks pop. It's a glorious night, the end of a glorious season.

Let's hope it turns out like that. If not my other fantasy, or should I say nightmare, may become reality.

In this, a certain columnist, smooth-talking and pretentious, makes a desperate dash for the station clutching his boots, a one-way ticket to the Shetlands and hotly pursued by 5,000 irate Reading supporters humming the Dead March - heaven forbid.

Gary Peters' winner at Darlington moved Reading up to third place, three points behind the leading pair of Lincoln and Northampton and three points ahead of fifth placed Huddersfield. The pace was fierce; the top four had won 32 out of a total 35 home games played. Three clubs had each drawn one game and won the rest but Reading had yet to drop a point at Elm Park.

"I don't remember us having a good home record at all. Plenty of draws I would have imagined. I was very conditioned to expect not to lose at home", recalls Eamon.

"We had a very good spirit, no nastiness or jealousy, some very good players and we did our stuff. Some of the players were better than Fourth Division. I didn't really think that far ahead but I could see a nucleus of a team that would do well in the Third."

"The great strength of the team was that it was well-organised and highly motivated. Only half a dozen in each division were. By well-organised I mean you make best sense of the available material and you need to identify what strengths a side should have and play to those strengths."

A fellow supporter recalls the playing style that season hazily but favourably. "They tried to play football, particularly Dunphy, he tried to pass the ball around. Most of the goals were good goals rather than the lucky goals we see today. Give the ball to Friday and he'd do it with Murray chipping in with some ridiculous goals from 30 yards. They were an entertaining side."

For the next game at home to Stockport Robin Friday returned and George Best, despite much speculation, stuck to his contract of only playing in County's home matches. It would have been an interesting comparison. Friday scored twice and Murray a hat-trick in a 5-0 win. The following week Murray got the winner against Scunthorpe as Reading established a new record of ten successive League home wins but it was not a match Dunphy enjoyed.

STINKER

EVENING POST, 20 DECEMBER 1975

Although we broke the record and gained two valuable points last Saturday was an unhappy day for me.

As those unfortunate enough to have witnessed the performance will testify, I had a stinker.

The first hint that it wasn't going to be my day should have been when my wife burnt the toast on which she presented her unique version of scrambled eggs. Alas, she does that every week!

No, the doubts first set in when I missed an open goal in the second minute of the game.

"Minty" set the chance up for me, or to be more precise for my left foot, an area of my anatomy over which I have very little control and which frequently declares UDI (Unilateral Declaration of Independence).

WORSE

Sadly worse was to follow. Determined to make good my mistake I desperately sought the ball and unfortunately got it. And gave it away again and again and again.

In fact I managed to find a Scunthorpe player with every second pass (a better average than our opponents achieved).

Still I plugged on embarrassingly. I mis-timed my tackles, played my colleagues into trouble, I called for the ball at the wrong time and made my biggest mistake by venturing into the vicinity of C Block where a fan reflected popular opinion by urging:

"Get your finger out you little fairy" (All I've got to say to him is... "Give us a kiss").

Professional opinion was on the whole, kinder to me. The other players didn't give me too hard a time. True Robin gave me some scornful looks and Bruce bellowed quite a bit, but taking into account the fact that I'm not slow to dish out stick to them on their off days they were lenient.

Dickie Rooks, Scunthorpe's manager, was heard to say afterwards "If we had 11 Eamonn Dunphy's we'd be in Europe." I wonder what he meant.

The boss has been very good. He hasn't mentioned Saturday to me - come to think of it he hasn't mentioned Tranmere either - or anything else.

THAT FEELING

Of course other pros know the feeling. They've all had their stinkers so they tend to be sympathetic. The public, on the other hand, are not so sympathetic and indeed why should they be? Standing in the Supporters Club enjoying my post-match pint of lager I was able to feel the cool draught of public opinion.

You know the feeling eyes are averted, heads shake, the old girl in the corner gives you a sympathetic wink "never mind luv".

You're like a man with your flies undone and no one knows how to tell you, except at a football club, where you will always get one.

Mine approached from a northerly direction, that is from behind.

He stood just outside my direct line of vision and out of the corner of my eye I watched him hesitate, composing, no doubt his shaft of wit. As it happens he wasn't very original but then they never are.

"Not so good today huh", it trickled out, accompanied by a sly knowing smile.

"Bet you don't know what I'm thinking, pig face" I thought while being content to smile benignly at him.

"Never mind eh," he threw over his shoulder as he moved off back to the darker corners of the club.

LEG-PULL

He really wasn't typical. In fact most people settled for some gentle leg-pulling such as that indulged in by my five friends behind the club bar who wouldn't give me a drink.

Hopefully most people will forgive me one stinker, as yet I haven't had too many for Reading, news that would surprise Millwall and Charlton fans who regularly had to hold their noses.

All in all it's not been a bad week considering. Little annoyances like finding my kit in the Oxford Road, not being told where the first team are training and having the departure time for Tranmere kept secret from me, can only be expected after such a performance.

And after all we did win, which is a bit of a feat with ten men!

Inevitably attention in a League club focuses on the deeds of the first team.

And while it's true to say that a club lives or dies on its Football League position, it is equally fair to observe that the long term welfare of a club rests in the hands of its youngsters.

NURSERY SUCCESS

Which brings us to Terry Knott and our nursery team, Reading I.T.S., who are enjoying considerable success in local competition.

They have reached the final of the Capelli Cup to be played at Palmer Park on Boxing Day morning. No mean feat when one considers that these 15 year-old lads have successfully taken on teams composed of 17 and 18 year-olds on the road to their little Wembley.

Terry whose good natured enthusiasm makes him ideally equipped for the delicate task of running such a side, tells me that he considers the club's youth scheme "the best for 29 years".

That happy situation, I know, delights the boss who will be at Palmer Park as, indeed, will some of our pros.

Unfortunately I will be eating burnt toast in preparation for the afternoon game against Cambridge, but if you've eaten too much turkey and finished playing with your kid's Christmas presents why not forego your wife's burnt toast and give the lads some support.

It will mean a lot to the kids, and who knows what you might be calling them in years to come.

Finally to all who read this column and those who don't - have a lovely Christmas.

Unbeaten in nine league games Reading, with Dunphy still in his customary number 10 shirt, travelled to Tranmere the Friday night before Christmas. A win would give Reading, in third place, a six point lead over fourth placed Tranmere and commentators would talk about the top three as a breakaway group.

In the event they were well beaten 2-0. They were never really in touch with Graham Taylor's league leaders, Lincoln City, again.

I remember leaving, intermittently, a 21st birthday party in a pub on the Gosbrook Road in Reading to phone for the latest bad news scoreline. Whenever I see that call box, these days very occasionally, I always think of that result. Can't remember a thing about the party.

Cambridge were beaten at Elm Park on Boxing Day and the following day a large support travelled down the M4 to Brentford. As ever the clash with the Bees was fractious and, as ever, Reading enjoyed their customary slice of fortune. Two down with quarter of an hour to go, completely outplayed, Peters scores with a header, Cumming is sent off for fighting. Reading throw in a barnstorming finish and when all seems lost Stuckey whacks in the equaliser - direct from a corner! The delicious injustice that seems to belong to a genuine promotion contender!

At the season's half way point the top of Division Four looked like this:

	P	W	D	L	W	D	L	F	A	PTS
Lincoln	22	10	1	0	7	2	2	55	24	37
Northampton	23	10	1	0	6	3	3	36	17	36
Reading	23	11	0	0	3	5	4	41	24	33
Tranmere	23	11	1	0	2	3	6	51	28	30
Bournemouth	21	8	2	2	3	3	3	29	14	27
Huddersfield	22	5	2	3	6	3	3	26	21	27

Promotion contenders didn't drop home points willy-nilly in them days!

350 UP

Every Saturday we sit in the bath eagerly awaiting the results in the hope that Lincoln or Northampton have been beaten.

The news, when it comes, is usually bad, so it was nice this week to be able to make our own news. The Northampton game also gave us a chance to measure ourselves against the best in the division.

It's been a strange season in the Fourth Division with the dominance of the leading four teams giving the League table a lopsided look.

Unlike the higher divisions, where for instance Crystal Palace have lost three times running to lowly opponents and Sunderland too have been prone to poor spells, ourselves, Lincoln and Northampton have rarely been threatened.

STRENGTH

The absence of real strength in depth can have a bearing on the promotion contenders for it may mean a higher than usual points total being needed to go up.

I fancy Huddersfield and Doncaster as most likely to challenge the present top four with Tranmere by virtue of their poor away form the most likely to collapse.

They have won only one point from their last five away games a statistic that points to some weakness of morale which will become more apparent when the going gets tougher....

My view of our chance remains unchanged - I think we're certainties.

To say such a thing in this game is to tempt fate but in view of the club's strengths it would be dishonest to say otherwise.

There is quality everywhere you look - players, management, coaching, potential and if proof of courage is needed the Brentford game bears testimony to that.

We should be thinking in terms of winning the championship rather than of surviving in the top four.

As a betting man I consider the 7-1 offer at the local betting shop as the best way of getting your holiday money - honestly.

What about Lincoln you rightly ask?

When we played them we were the better team for an hour and led 1-0 but such was their belief in themselves that, inspired by their fervent supporters, they fought back to win.

It was an immensely impressive performance and an accurate reflection of a club that has about it an air of confidence rarely found at this level of the game.

Graham Taylor, their young manager, must take the credit for not only revitalising the team but for going out into the town to forge a link between club and community that stands as an example to every club in the League, but particularly to those in the lower divisions where the game is dying for a lack of original managerial ideas.

In practical terms Lincoln take the game to the people. Visits are arranged to schools and factories, players are active in the town, communicating something of themselves and their lives to those who come to support them.

In recognising the importance of the club-community relationship Lincoln have created interest and goodwill in a part of the country where little football tradition exists.

And, in these cost-conscious days, at no great expense.

It is a superb achievement about which one can really say that "I have seen the future and it works."

Of course I still think we'll hammer them at Elm Park 'cos we've got Robin!

From the Department of Statistics came the news that today's match against Northampton was my 350th League game.

And I can honestly say it meant more to me than any of its 349 predecessors.

Three hundred and fifty is not a particularly significant number - quite puny in fact when laid alongside the 700-odd appearances of Terry Paine, or the many players who reach the 500 mark.

What 350 suggests is a talent for modest survival, less than one would have hoped for as a starry-eyed 15-year-old but enough to earn the gratitude of a 30-year-old veteran.

I hesitate to used the word veteran for at the risk of sounding cliched, I've never felt better nor enjoyed my football more.

DANGEROUS AGE

But of course, when one arrives at football's "dangerous age", 30, the pen pictures begin to be sprinkled with new words - "veteran", "experienced", "vastly experienced", "wily old campaigner", "durable".

Thus one is described with words more suitable to a venerable old family retainer, the implication being that the glory days will soon be over.

How quickly one moves through the football ages from "promising youngster" through "established pro" to "veteran campaigner"!

If one were to last until 35 the label "credit to the game" would be stuck on, however unwarranted.

In reality the labels are meaningless. You can be young and unpromising, an old campaigner and stupid, 35 and an absolute disgrace to football.

PRESSURES

This categorising of players creates its own subtle pressures. If one constantly reads of oneself as being a "veteran" does not one begin to feel old?

I really feel that this is so and explains why many players finish long before their time.

Conventional wisdom may tag a player as old at 30 but one has only to look at Terry Paine or Frank McLintock and many others to see the folly of such thinking.

The secret of football longevity lies in ignoring the insidious pressures that surround the dangerous age. To a large extent ageing is a state of mind - you're only as old as you think.

Personally I am more interested in the future and I fully intend to go on playing as long as I enjoy the game. To this end I have taken a course for older players which gave some hints on how to ensure a ripe old age.

GESTURES

There are five basic suggestions that I freely offer to those in similar circumstances:

1. Be nice to your manager.

2. Make small gestures, i.e. clean his car, carry his case on away trips.

3. Compliment him on his five-a-side form. However sycophantic this may seem, however untrue, he will believe you.

4. Keep up front on training runs. If it ever gets too hard complain of tummy trouble (common to young and old).

5. Never remember his birthday. Most of them like to believe they're 27 and don't take kindly to the harsh facts.

Following that advice there's no reason why you too can't become a veteran.

And what of the individual matches that go to make up the 350 league appearances, the essential atoms of a footballer's working life? We looked through the 1975/76 fixture list. What does Eamon recall?

"Scunthorpe? No. Barnsley, Bradford? No. No. Newport away I do remember, it was a midweek fixture, they were struggling really badly and we beat them I think. I remember that night, it was such a dilapidated place. There was an air of awfulness about it. We win?"

"No, it was 0-0."

"We beat Doncaster, didn't we?"

"No, it was a draw."

"I remember that match because it was a good pitch. Torquay away I do remember. They didn't score against us. Death played very well that night."

"I'm not a great one for remembering matches. John Giles can tell you about every single match he ever played in. I can think of about three or four from my Millwall days, like Norwich, a cup game against Everton at Goodison."

Reading beat Northampton 1-0 with a goal from centre-half Geoff Barker in front of 10,000 at Elm Park. The next week, in terrible storms and gales, we travelled to Southport, who were well clear at the bottom of the table, still without a home win and with only five points all season.

On the coach we had a guess-the-gate sweep. Their crowds were so small you could virtually work it out. Alas, I wasn't the only one to come up with the exact winning figure of 1,167. Playing into the gale Reading trailed 1-0 at half-time with the Sandgrounders playing as if their lives depended on it.

"Soutnport away? We win 1-0, 2-0?"

"2-1. Do you remember what happened in the last minute?"

"We either got a penalty or gave one away."

"You gave one away."

"Me, personally. For doing what?" bridled Eamon.

"Calm down, you won't get out of it now."

"It was pissing down that day. That I do remember now. I had terrible trouble with my back. I was dying. That was one of the worst days of pain in my life".

"Deathie saved it."

"Good old Deathie, no wonder I liked him. All these games, they tend to blur into one. I must have played six, seven or more times at Huddersfield. I'm afraid I'm very bad in terms of remembering the specifics."

Reading's new home record advanced further with a win over Workington (Cumming sent off again) but they were then struck by a surprise defeat at Watford.

ARTHUR HORSFIELD RUINED MY WEEKEND

EVENING POST, 31 JANUARY 1976

SATURDAY

Vicarage Road, a "lucky" ground for me. In all the games I've played there only once have I been on the losing side - with York City many moons ago.

Playing for Millwall I once scored from 30 yards - and meant it! So I feel reasonably confident about the game except for two nagging doubts. They're on song having won their last two games - 2-1 at Doncaster last week. Then there's the law of averages, perhaps my Watford luck's run out.

Still, every reason to hope that tonight we'll be top of the league and a long way clear of Bournemouth and Huddersfield. The absence of Gordon Cumming and "Minty" won't help our cause, but they've both come along to see the game.

As we're getting changed "Minty" comes in to tell us it's started to snow and at once 11 envious pairs of eyes focus on his nice warm sheepskin coat. There are days when the prospect of leaving the warmth of a centrally heated dressing room seems less than inviting - this is such a day.

TROUBLE

Within a couple of minutes of the start I'm in trouble. Stretching to clear the ball from our penalty area I aggravate an old back injury. There's nothing to be done, unless I want the world record for quitting the game, but it looks like a restricted "mid-field dynamo" for 88 minutes.

We're soon in control of things. Moving sweetly, playing good two touch football, and by half-time are unlucky not be a couple of goals up.

The second half continues in much the same way - a matter of time until we score. Sure enough Robin notches - that ought to be enough I'm confidently thinking. A rude shock awaits. From the re-start Watford win a free kick. The ball is cleared, knocked back again, deflected and Ross Jenkins sickens us.

Damn it - just the wrong time to let them back into it - if we could have held for five minutes we'd have been okay - now we've got a 25 minute scrap on our hands.

STRUGGLING

I'm struggling with my injury, so off I go leaving Gary Peters, a better defensive proposition, to take over.

Sitting on the bench we never sensed any real danger

in those last 25 minutes. The winner, when it came, was a surprise. Not the result of constant pressure, but an explosive moment that culminated in Arthur Horsfield thieving a last minute winner.

Stunned we sit silently in the dressing room. We're not used to losing and that makes it so much harder to take. There are no excuses, just despair in people's eyes, grim looks on the faces. The heavy unfamiliar gloom of defeat. In contrast the sounds of victory next door, laughing, cheering. Things at last looking up for Watford. Great!

Well that's the weekend ruined. It's a long seven days until next Saturday and Newport. Seven days to nurse your wounds, to recriminate silently with yourself, to ponder on what might - indeed ought - to have been and to stiffen your resolve, no more bloody defeats.

SUNDAY

Never read the papers after losing. Avoid the League table like the plague. The other contestants all won - well, of course, they would. The basic reason we all try so hard to win is to avoid this lousy losing feeling.

Today I stole a furtive glance at the Fourth Division table. Huddersfield with four games in hand 10 points behind. For a moment a twinge of fear, suppose they won them all and we started losing. No, bloody ridiculous. We're certainties. Reflecting on yesterday I'm convinced it was a freak result. We played well - did enough to win - but Watford quite simply took the only two chances they had.

Arthur Horsfield, talking afterwards, admitted that they'd been lucky. "Don't worry Eamonn lad, you'll be there at the finish." We will.

MONDAY

A day in bed with my back injury which is bad enough to cause me some doubt about being fit for Saturday. I've suffered back trouble for a couple of years and last season it nearly caused me to finish playing.

I have been fortunate to find relief through a course of acupuncture treatment and by and large have enjoyed a trouble-free season so far. Now it looks like more needles but that's a small price to pay for being fit to play.

TUESDAY

Treatment under the soothing hands of Jimmy Wallbanks. It's very pleasant in Jim's treatment room. Nice and warm, a cup of tea from old Bill. Death's Sporting Life and Jim's stories.

A man could grow to like it in there, much better than the cold, harsh winds of the training ground.

The problem, particularly for veterans, is that missing training means losing condition which in turn leads to more injuries - a vicious circle - so tomorrow I've got to get off my backside!

WEDNESDAY

I'm back on parade to be greeted with cheers and derision - "welcome back" my friends mock. In the icy wind it's hardly a pleasure but there's good news for Gordon.

He's got off with a lenient suspension of one game which only goes to prove that British justice is alive and well and living at Lancaster Gate. How can people say unkind things about the FA.

"Minty", my fellow member of "Wally's Treatment Room Club" is still struggling with a fractured foot.

THURSDAY

Prospect Park for a friendly game, with the boss and Maurice Evans taking part. Once again both on the losing side and one can't help feeling how sad it is to see once great players in their twilight years.

The weather is not funny, how one longs for the warmth of Wally's Room or even a cup of Bill's tea - things are desperate.

One man undaunted by the weather is Robin. Exuberant as ever he even volunteered to travel as 12th man with the reserves to Crystal Palace on Wednesday. He looks ominously sharp this week - I'm glad I don't play for Newport!

Acupuncture Day for me which means also a heavenly massage, manipulations and half an hour with needles protruding everywhere. It's good stuff and should ensure a new, improved product on Saturday.

FRIDAY

The great thing about the club at the moment is how determined everyone is to cancel out any defeat. Our pride is offended and one can sense the indignation of last week's result and the resolve to put matters right tomorrow. That professional pride is really our strongest weapon.

The next game, at home to Newport County, was postponed. Sometimes a postponement can destroy a team's momentum as effectively as a defeat. There is no reason to suspect Newport would have inflicted any blemish on a still perfect home record of thirteen straight wins.

For the first time in the season Reading had to play three consecutive away league matches - and lost them all, starting with that result at Watford.

A fortnight later, the Biscuitmen as they were then still known, were thrashed 5-1 at Swansea with youngsters Alan Curtis and Robbie James on the scoresheet.

For Eamon's sceptical readers, too, it was a harrowing time.

A DANGEROUS TIME FOR ALL OF US

EVENING POST, 14 FEBRUARY 1976

There's no such thing as a smooth, crisis-free promotion challenge.

At some point in the nine month marathon every team experiences a setback, even a disaster, and it is the ability to cope with the crisis that sorts out the eventual promotion winners.

Our 5-1 defeat at Swansea heralds our moment of truth.

Our reaction to that defeat and to the severe challenge of the next few weeks will settle the promotion issue. In simple terms - we will get what we deserve.

If we've got the faith, the courage and the character in sufficient measure we'll be alright. If not we'll be found out.

It is a dangerous time for all of us. You find your emotions at once touched with fear and yet tingling with anticipation at the challenge of the days ahead.

COMPETITION

It is a time when a player, or club can galvanise themselves to meet the challenger or crumble beneath the strain. That in the end is what competition is all about, the difference between winners and losers.

One of the fascinating things about football is the reaction of people in and around a club under strain. You can see men grow to meet the demands of the time, others hesitate, looking for a lead, and always lurking around the moaners who seem to thrive on other people's failure.

"He should have done this" or "that". "I knew all along they wouldn't do it."

In such circumstances leadership is crucial - a source of strength for the hesitant - a rock on which the petty-minded founder.

Although they won't thank me for saying so (the lads, too, will give me stick for crawling), the boss and Maurice Evans have done a marvellous job of picking us off the floor this week. The pressure on them is even more acute, yet their obvious faith in us, as individuals and as a side has kept morale high when it could so easily have been dissolved.

MAINTAINED

They have maintained a good, professional, working atmosphere, a feat not easily managed in the aftermath of a 5-1 defeat.

Despite the fact that we're all uneasy - and will be until the next two points - there has been no panic, no scapegoats *and no recriminations. Common sense - often the first casualty in defeat - tells us that the players and principles and third place in the table haven't been devalued in a fortnight.*

There's some consolation in the fact that we weren't alone in our troubles last weekend.

For instance Derby conceded four goals at Newcastle, Huddersfield lost at home, Northampton dropped a home point and Lincoln lost at Tranmere. Sunderland, too, lost at Fulham and Leeds are also in the middle of a losing spell.

PRESSURES

At this stage of the season the pressures of being front runners begins to take its toll, particularly for sides who've been up there since August.

Coincidentally it's also the time when "Springers" - mid-table sides under no pressure - catch fire. Relaxed, with nothing to lose, your "springer" is a dangerous animal, especially on his home ground. Swansea come into this category as do Leicester in the First Division and Wrexham in the Third. They are the sides that usually finish the season with a flourish and everybody says "watch them next year".

Alas "next year" never comes. Flatterers who live to deceive, but heaven help you if you catch them on song.

Alongside this column the Evening Post ran the headline "Hurley's new plan misfires" as Reading went down 4-1 at Exeter. Bruce Stuckey was carried off, the first of a series of long-term casualties.

"Exeter away I remember. It was a lovely, balmy night. I only played there once. I remember going down on the coach. We got beat, I don't know why. We were under a lot pressure down the hill there and we spent a lot of time trying to get the ball up it."

Reading's season was in a vale of darkness. They actually dropped a home point for the first time on 21 February to Torquay in a goalless draw.

For the match at home to Hartlepool Murray was dropped in favour of Whitham, once more, Hetzke replaced Barker at centre half and Dunphy was on the bench with local youngster Adrian Cooper in his place.

"Jesus, I must have committed some horrific disciplinary offence", he exclaimed when reminded.

For Cumming nothing had gone right since being made captain. He was injured in the game, had a cartilage operation and played only two more matches that season.

Like the Torquay game the match against Hartlepool was terrible but Friday scored a second half winner to put Reading back into third place. Now, though, both Tranmere and Huddersfield could catch them by winning games in hand.

There was little more Eamon could add to his previous column over this fortnight so he gave advice to his football-obsessed son and offered his views on the First Division Championship race.

A wretched 3-0 defeat at closest challengers Huddersfield followed. It was the fourth successive away defeat and nobody but Friday had scored for seven games. Our momentum had stopped. This was exactly the kind of result in seasons gone by that signalled the customary slither down to sixth place. As far as I was concerned that was what was going to happen. I was despairing, fed-up and not going to away games.

Eamon heard the same concerns from different sources and did not ignore them in his next column.

THE FEAR THAT HAUNTS THIS TOWN

EVENING POST, 6 MARCH 1976

"Reading Football Club and promotion to the Third Division - is this just a dream or reality?"

That question, posed in an interesting letter from this week's post, reflects the anxiety felt by many of our supporters after our recent disastrous spell.

The letter from one of the 400 supporters who made the tiring fruitless journey to Huddersfield last Saturday was hard hitting but on the whole fair and the points raised deserve an answer.

As one of my optimistic mid-season quotes was resurrected (as I feared it would if the going got tough) perhaps I ought to respond.

Essentially what the writer Mr Beggs was saying was *"let's be honest"*. Well let's try.

RIGHT

He says of the Huddersfield performance *"there were no heads held high, no grit to get into the game, in fact nothing to suggest anything other than the fact that we shall all be watching Fourth Division football again next season."*

There was, says Mr Beggs, *"A lack of character and commitment."*

I think he is just about right. Our performance against Huddersfield was the worst this season and the conclusions drawn by Mr Beggs and indeed all those who travelled there are an accurate reading of the game.

We felt ashamed travelling back on that train acutely conscious that 400 people had spent time and money to support us and we had let them down badly. Seeing the hurt on the kids' faces, the perplexed looks on their dads' was every bit as painful as losing two points.

Let's be honest? Well, there's no excuse for our performance, but there has to be an explanation. Is it *"lack of character and commitment"* or is it a question of morale being shattered by a string of alarming away defeats?

If we lack the necessary character then we wouldn't be in third place in the table nor would we have averaged a point a game away from home up to the Watford game.

I believe it's a question of morale, which isn't to deny the validity of Mr Beggs' point. When morale is low you need to dig deep into your character to find the guts necessary to get a result away from home. No one could dispute the fact that on that count last Saturday we were guilty.

We've got six more away games which will in effect decide our fate. I don't believe we will let promotion slip for lack of guts.

But, of course, it's no use writing it down. We can't afford any more Huddersfields.

Mr Beggs goes on to plead "Please no excuses this time". Again he's absolutely right in principle, although I think it's an over-simplification to label all explanations as excuses.

The point about excuses is well worth making. It is tempting as a player to excuse oneself a bad performance by blaming anything from the bumpy pitch to the mother-in-law's burnt toast. We're all prone, particularly your columnist, whose friends have been known to fall asleep listening to the bumpy pitch theory, but of course, it is unprofessional and no help at all towards putting things right.

FACT

However, it is necessary to analyse defeats and if having done so honestly one then offers an explanation to the public is that an "excuse"?

I can assure you that anyone offering excuses in our dressing room these days is assured of a rough ride.

Still I think it's reasonable to argue that "every team hits a bad patch" etc as long as you don't believe that by offering an explanation you are curing the problem.

So what is wrong?

Quite simply there are too many of us playing below form. That's not an excuse - it's an unpalatable fact.

What can be done?

Well there's no miracle cure for loss of form. If there was there would be medals for all. You can only work as hard as you can, put your head down and battle your way through. That sounds uncomfortably like a cliche. Unfortunately it's just about true as well.

When it happens at this time of year it's particularly difficult to cope with. There's enough pressure without worrying about where your next through ball will land you.

(I'm beginning to make excuses).

PROBLEMS

What it boils down to is this. With 13 games to go we've got problems. But we're not alone, a fact that because of Reading's history, is very often forgotten. Every side in the race for honours have or have had their own particular problems. What makes ours seem worse is the timing. Yet consider some of the others not as a means of excusing ours, simply in order to put them in perspective.

Bolton lost at home to Oxford on Wednesday night. Sunderland like ourselves can't get a result away from home. Southampton have lost two away games this week, one at lowly York. That's just the Second Division.

Crystal Palace have won two of their last 11 League games. Brighton can't get anything away from home. Peterborough lost at home last week. That's the problem in the Third Division. Not to mention mighty Leeds, who have managed a paltry one point from their last three home games.

We are, of course, only interested in our own fate but I think it helps occasionally to look around if only to recognise that the road to promotion is not all downhill.

There is, however, one line in Mr Beggs' letter with which I fundamentally disagree, where he talks of seeing "a team write off their promotion hopes". Nothing betrays more the fear that haunts this town and the burden of living with the failures of the past.

NONSENSE

To talk of a team in our position as having "written off" hope of promotion is quite frankly "bloody nonsense". There's no excuse for that either.

We've got a fantastic chance of going up, despite the shocks of recent weeks.

There's no justification for excuses, nor indeed for last Saturday, but neither is there for those, who with 13 games to go, want to chuck the towel in because "they've seen it all before".

I don't give a damn for history and I don't see why the present side should be burdened with what's past.

If in six weeks time we've failed then we'll all be judged. Until then we'll be too busy to think about the past - coping with the present.

A final thought. If someone had said to me at the beginning of the season that we'd be in our present position with 13 games to go I'd have fancied our chances. I still do.

Fans and players were locked into a set of expectations that they were beginning to realise might not happen. Sometimes a bad defeat signals 'the end of the world', sometimes it doesn't. One excuse Dunphy could and didn't use was the injury to Steve Death. He played on despite breaking his jaw at a forward's feet, but that game was the end of his season. John Turner ably deputised thereafter.

But even now Eamon insists that there was no real crisis.

"A run like that is serious but it was never a panic situation. We knew there weren't many better sides than us."

"You do begin to doubt a little bit, but nothing more than that. There was never any danger of us not going up if we kept our heads."

"There were no fights in the dressing room or loss of morale. If you're a strong side you ought to know what's wrong and how to put it right. If you're a weak side you don't know where to start."

A Murray penalty defeated Newport in the re-arranged fixture. Hurley's programme notes for the next game against Doncaster caught the edginess of the time.

"I know that you, our fans, get frustrated with the football we are playing as compared with the way we were playing before Christmas", the manager wrote. "But you are still coming to watch. You 6,000 have stuck by us - and we appreciate this very much."

"I know some give us the bird, but as long as you keep coming we do not mind what you do because we need all the support you can give us. If a footballer (whether he is a manager or a player) cannot take a bit of stick he should not be in the game."

Almost inevitably, it seemed, Doncaster then broke Reading's unbeaten home record with their fifth successive away win. Fifth placed Huddersfield were only four points behind with three games in hand. Northampton and Lincoln at the top were leaving a large gap behind them. Fatalism was rife.

Hurley reached for the Chairman's cheque book and Mick Butler, the Barnsley centre-forward. Ominously, Huddersfield signed him instead. Just before the deadline he plunged, not too strong a word, for Dennis Nelson of Crewe (£10,000) and Mick Hollis of Stockport County (£4,000). They took the places of Murray and Hiron in an encouraging draw at Bradford City.

FIRST SIGHTING OF AN ALTERNATIVE VIEW

EVENING POST, 13 MARCH 1976

Speculation all week. New signings in the air. Curiosity in the dressing room - who was coming? - whose place would be lost? - what effect on our performances?

The psychological boost of new faces is much needed - on that we all agree.

The arrival of new players begs other, very important questions. For instance can they play "nine-card brag"? are they "tapable" for shampoo, fags, 50p (until Friday)?

Will they join the post-game drinks "whip"? Be useful allies in five-a-side warfare? Fascinating questions.

LOSS

Monday's draw for the FA cup semi-finals was bad news for those who had looked forward to a Derby-Manchester United final. I am firmly on the side of those who mourn the loss of what could have been a memorable football occasion.

And the prospect of enduring the "Big Mal" show all the way to Wembley hardly eases the pain. The Allison of the late 60's, early 70's brilliant coach, provocative thinker, now fades from memory. In his place a loud, boastful, ego-tripper more Bertram Mills than Don Quixote.

The more he boasts the more pressure he puts on his team, which, while reasonably competent, is far from capable of living up to the claims "Big Mal" makes on their behalf.

It is I think fair to say that the saturation coverage the media affords to pro-football tends to encourage our belief in our own self importance.

Our daily diet of football news has a high hysteria content. The words and thoughts of "Big Mal" or "Big Mac" assume earth-shattering importance, despite their overwhelming banality - there is little in the way of light relief for those who browse through the sports pages.

FOUL

Therefore the emergence a couple of years ago of "Foul", a satirical football paper, was most welcome.

Started by a group of football loving Cambridge undergrads "Foul" regards itself as an "alternative" football paper.

"Alternative" that is to the everyday nonsense that passes in many popular papers for "sports coverage".

"Foul" is irreverent, in very bad taste and very refreshing.

It has not taken the world by storm - distribution is a problem, as, indeed, is the variable quality of it contributors

*- but it survives and deservedly so for all its minority appeal.
They have just published "Foul Book of Football" which
incorporates the best of the paper over its brief lifespan.*

*"Norma Huntress", "Aston Villans", the "Foul" awards for
"clogging" are just a few of the regulars included along with
a fair sprinkling of the type of hard news stories Fleet Street
wouldn't print.*

The following is typical of the "Foul" sense of humour.

*"During the 1973/74 season, a group of professional
footballers were nearing the end of a long training session on
a little ground near Cheshunt. As they knelt down to do some
press-ups, one of the players, a young apprentice
professional, took out a deck of cards.*

*"Put away those cards you horrible little Tommy Baldwin"
screamed the coach. After the training session was over, the
apprentice was put on the transfer list and brought before the
manager.*

*The boss said: "Eddy, why have you brought this
longhaired lout into my nice carpeted managerial suit?"*

*"For playing cards in training, Mr Nicholson." The Boss
looked at the apprentice and said, "I hope you have an
explanation."*

*And the apprentice said: "Sir, I've been sweating my
guts out all morning. I had no Daily Mirror and no midday
edition of the Standard, but I had these cards.*

*"You see, sir, when I see the ACE, I am reminded that
there is but one Sir Alf, Lord and Master over all."*

*"When I see the DEUCE, it reminds me that football is
divided into two parts, the Football Association and the
Football League."*

*"And when I see the THREES I think of our beloved
match officials."*

*"When I see the FOUR I think of the Russian linesman
and the four goals he allowed England in the World Cup
final."*

*"The FIVE reminds me of the London Clubs. There are
ten in all - five in the First Division and five in the Second and
Third. Oh and Brentford."*

*"When I see the SIX, it reminds me of the six yard box,
and I wonder what it's for."*

*"When I see the SEVEN, I think of the seven goals which
England's heroes put past the mighty Austrians as a prelude
to World Cup glory."*

*"When I see the EIGHT I think of the righteous fans'
attitude towards Nottingham Forest. We eight Nottingham
Forest."*

*"And when I see the NINE, I think of the shirt, that, years
before, Alf KNEW Bobby Charlton would wear in the 1966
World Cup."*

"I see the TEN and I think of the number of years Martin Peters is ahead of his time."

The KING reminds me of the Millwall goalkeeper, when I see the four QUEENS I think of the West Ham defence and the Knave or Jack is manager of Middlesbrough."

"When I see the SPOTS on a deck of cards, I am reminded of the unacceptable face of Charlie George."

"There are FIFTY-TWO cards in a pack, the number of goals scored by P. Hubbard of Grimsby Town in his whole career."

"There are four suits, HEARTS the famous Scottish side. CLUBS of which there are 92 in the Football League. DIAMONDS which studded the notorious Bobby Moore bracelet in Bogota, and SPADES who make up most of West Ham's forward line."

"You see, Boss, my deck of cards has served me as my Rothman's Football Yearbook, my fixture list and my FA Book of Rules."

And the Apprentice was given a testimonial.

Eamon, like myself, had been a contributor to 'Foul'. He recalls its role in the Seventies.

"Basically 'Foul' was a reaction against bad sports writing. Journalism has its own agenda and it doesn't reflect the real agenda that players and fans have."

"The fans perspective on the game is incorrect. Journalism should link the players and the fans but it doesn't. In France and the U.S. sports journalism is better therefore there is no need for such magazines."

"The existence of fanzines is a terrible reflection on the standards of journalism. But people in the game can and will ignore fanzines."

We were both surprised it took another ten to fifteen years for fanzines to catch on. Interestingly, there are very few other examples of a professional footballer endorsing or encouraging them, which says something of the pact between football and media men and their views of the fans' views.

Meanwhile, back in the Seventies, Reading were unchanged at home to Barnsley, a game they had to win to stay in the top four. They started well, couldn't score, started kicking, lost their way and finished struggling amid the cat-calls. 0-0 and down to fifth place on goal average from both Tranmere and Huddersfield.

THE WORLD REDUCED TO JUST THREE TEAMS

EVENING POST, 20 MARCH 1976

THURSDAY MORNING, 10AM

Blank pages waiting to be filled,
With bright and witty prose,
Of how last night I thrilled
The fans by vanquishing the foe.
Of course, the problem with last night,
The script didn't turn out quite right,
Barnsley came and spoilt the fun,
Imagine, they held us to none-none.
Outstanding memory of the night?
When boredom reached its height,
A wag from on the terrace high,
Sung out a bitter, mocking cry.
"Hang your boots up, Dunphy, now,
You're past it, like the rest"
And though I pretended not to hear,
I felt it somewhere in my chest.

ECHOES

Now it echoes in my ears,
As do so many other jeers
Sourness from a night of scorn,
Hanging over Thursday morn,
The column I had planned this week,
Was witty, bright, rather sleek,
This morning I don't really care,
If Allison goes to Wembley bare,
Or Dougan sponsors Playtex Bras,
Rodney Marsh defects to Mars,
Man United win the Double,
Or Stanley Bowles gets into trouble.
Supremely unimportant now,
The latest "shock" "horror" "walk out" row,
Amazing how fussed we get,
When poor old Stanley has a bet!
The issue now is nearer home,
Right in deep, along the bone,
The world reduced to just three teams,
Tranmere, Reading, and Huddersfield.

BLISS

The original script was not like this,
It was a tale of endless bliss,
Of triumph starring Robert Redford,
This is more like David Bedford.
I knew we'd have our toil and troubles,
In this game life never simply bubbles,
But after Saturday at Bradford,
I'd begun to feel once more like Redford.
Justice it seemed would yet be done,
The war eventually won.
The tribulations all worth while,
Reading celebrating with a smile,
Some now say it can't be done,
Our efforts a mere source of fun.
The knives are posed to leave the sheaths,
A touch of the Old Ted Heaths.
Temptation now is all around,
To cause no stir, to make no sound,
To leave the stage unobtrusively,
To clear the decks for Calvary.
No hero wants to be a man,
When the "whatsit" hits the fan,
We all love credit, fame and glory,
Alas in failure it's a different story.
But wait a minute, have we failed?
Has the ship really sailed?
Are we quitting far too soon?
Could it just be a cloud passing o'er the moon?
We've got ten more games to go.
A lot of water still to flow.
We're still the guardians of our fate,
It's not by any means too late.

THEORIES

To say so on this miserable morn,
Invites a flow of crushing scorn,
"The man is simply talking corn,
Was a greater con-man ever born?"
Is this the time for tales of woe,
For fallow seeds of doubt to sow?
Or is it time to stand and fight,
Whether wrong or whether right?
We've all got theories of what's been wrong,
Our own particular favourite song,
If only X were moved to Y,
If only earth bound pigs could fly.
Mutter, Mutter, Mumble, Moan,
Grumble, Gripe, Gesticulate and Groan,
Panic piercing every pore,

Fate is knocking on the door,
Put aside desire to doubt,
To panic-stricken, bawl and shout,
Hysterics never won a thing,
Ranting has a hollow ring.
Other random thoughts today,
Of mortgages and debts to pay,
My wife has just spent fifty pounds,
Her optimism knows no bounds.
Think of hefty bonus lost,
But that is not the real cost,
You pay in shattered pride,
In glorious dreams destroyed,
In trust betrayed,
In kids dismayed,
In fans who paid,
And stayed, and stayed,
Standing in the cold outside,
A nipper, sorry, sad, red-eyed,
His favour torn, cast aside,
The wreckage of a dream that died.
That's what it's really all about,
For us who play, and you who shout,
Hope and joy, frustration, fears,
Winning, losing, cursing, tears.

The players were on a 'hefty' quarterly bonus paid if, after 12, 24, 36 and 46 games, they were in the top four. Some of the crowd were aware of this and wondered whether that was behind the desperation and violence on the pitch. Eamon denied the suspicion.

"We weren't a kicking side really. If you go through that side Dave Moreline would kick people, very bitey in the tackle, Geoff wouldn't kick anyone, that was part of our problem, Tommy Youlden didn't really kick, Stewart Henderson didn't kick, that's for sure, Gary Peters didn't even get close enough to kick them..." (Peters and Dunphy, it should be pointed out did actually "make contact" in a training session some time later and the animosity lived on). I would have to take issue about that night's performance. They laid in to Barnsley in a way that I found embarrassing as a supporter.

But three days later the sun came back out on Reading's season. For the first time in twelve games they scored more than one goal. Darlington were crushed 4-1 at Elm Park on a bright afternoon when goals, suddenly, were easy to come by and the fans could relax again. In their next game Reading drew away at Stockport County.

Bobby Collins had resigned as manager of

Huddersfield and they had begun to lose first at home to Barnsley then heavily away at Exeter. But they were still only a point behind Reading when Tranmere arrived at Elm Park for a real four-pointer. Defeat for either side would still leave Huddersfield masters of their own fate.

As Clive Thomas blew for kick-off the teams were positioned thus:

		Played	Points
1.	Lincoln	36	57
2.	Northampton	39	57
3.	Tranmere	38	49
4.	Reading	38	49
5.	Huddersfield	38	48

VERY IMPORTANT

EVENING POST, 26 MARCH 1976

A good night's work? A point away from home is always welcome, but we should have had two at Stockport.

We didn't play particularly well yet managed to score three goals, two of which were disallowed for reasons that remain mysterious.

What is there left to say about the standard of refereeing? We simply must learn to live with the problem, frustrating as it is at times.

I had my name taken for dissent, my second booking in three seasons.

Over the years my disciplinary record has improved as experience has taught me the futility of arguing with "officials". I have seen the weirdest decisions, for and against, and now nothing surprises me.

The "booking" cost me a fiver fine levied by the boss which goes into the "kitty" for our end of season booze-up.

We travelled to Stockport by coach and the journey proved to be eventful. Our drivers Brian and Melvyn provided the "cabaret". Brian helped to relieve the pre-match tension by giving Mel the wrong directions but Mel got his own back by doing likewise to Brian when he took over as navigator.

Still, they took the abuse in the right spirit with Brian pointing out that he gets his laughs watching us play. Bob, our regular driver, was ill. Here's wishing him a speedy recovery. Come back Bob all is forgiven!

All good fun, which is more than I can say for the card school. I am learning the expensive way that three-card brag is yet another game I can't play and on this trip I "did" three weeks bonus. To Mrs Moreline, Murray, Hiron, etc., if you've noticed your husbands spending freely of late, don't thank them, thank me.

SATURDAY

More losses on the ITV Seven and the Lincoln Handicap proves as much a mystery to me as that map proved for Mel and Brian. Time to "relax" whilst waiting for the Exeter-Huddersfield result. The news is good. Can I afford a celebratory pint tonight?

SUNDAY

The papers. Big Mal, Fiona Richmond and foul play at Shepherds Bush.

The more one reads of Big Mal and life at Crystal Palace the more one is reminded of a Harold Robbins novel. Sex, blood pressures, money, even occasionally some football.

Terry Venables (the second greatest coach on the planet) co-stars.

The supporting roles taken by Alan (I can't stop being sick) Whittle, Peter (best left-winger in the country) Taylor, and a host of bit players too numerous to mention. Fascinating stuff. What will life be like if they ever win anything!

To date Big Mal's achievement has been to take Palace down two divisions. Still why quibble when we're having fun.

The QPR-Manchester City punch-up was unfortunate. Rangers are on the verge of a spectacular triumph that can only be marred by the kind of brawling witnessed on Sunday.

It is held against them that they have accumulated enough disciplinary points to anchor them at the foot of the Fair Play League, whatever that is. That this is so tells you more about the inadequacies of the disciplinary system than about Rangers' disposition. They are not a dirty side.

The thing that bothers me about the disciplinary system and, for that matter about fair play leagues, is that they never reveal the real villains which must surely be the object of the exercise.

MONDAY

Hello, it's Mal again! This time feuding with Millwall's Gordon Jago. Has Jago been secretly dating Fiona Richmond?

Have Millwall tried to sign her behind Mal's back? Or is the "Big Man" simply drumming up ticket sales for tomorrow's derby game? Who cares.

TUESDAY

"The greatest Third Division side ever" drew 0-0 at home to Millwall.

Thirty-eight thousand people are parted from £20,000 - £8,000 worth of ancillaries, scarves, badges, nude photos of Fiona, etc., sold.

Not bad for a Third Division game considering that QPR a few miles away can, whilst topping the First Division, only lure 20,000 to watch them. The message must clearly be "Get your clothes off Dave and give Fiona a ring."

WEDNESDAY

Tranmere. Very important, they all are now. We got the break we needed with two first half penalties which, in effect, ended the game as a contest.

They threw everything into attack in the second half and had they pulled a goal back it could have been a battle. But Robin's magnificent volley sealed their fate and thereafter the game was pretty false. We turned it on but you don't have to be a great player to play when you're 3-0 up.

The really pleasing feature of the game was Ray Hiron's performance. Ray's had the kind of spell that all of us dread and inevitably suffer. Confidence drained, fate conspiring to *sell you "dummies". We've all been through it, yet few have coped as bravely as Ray. He's never "hidden", never stopped trying, and earned respect from the fans and from us as well.*

THURSDAY

Mixed news from the sick bay. Gordon Cumming has made a swift recovery following his cartilage operation and hopes to be back training next week.

Bruce Stuckey has not been so fortunate and now learns that he must have a hernia operation.

They've both shown great courage in facing the kind of situation we all have nightmares about.

They have to endure not only the loneliness of the solitary fight for fitness but the frustration of missing the climax of a successful season to which both have made major contributions.

Gordon seems certain to be back before the end of the month but for Bruce it looks like a summer-long battle for fitness. If it's any consolation Bruce you've played your last game in the Fourth Division.

FRIDAY

On the road again. This time to Rochdale. Several important questions to be answered. Can we get two points?

Can I avoid bankruptcy? Will Brian and Mel solve the riddle of the M1?

What surprises will the man in black spring on us? And of course will Big Mal get to Wembley?

What part will Fiona play in the build up?

Still living in South East London was clearly distracting Eamon from the importance of Reading's achievement! Forget Fiona. What about Tranmere?

It was Reading's night. 5-0. Murray 3 (2 pens) Friday 2. For the fans it was the highlight of the season and the best League result for six years. The pro was more dispassionate both then and now.

"The referee made a complete balls of it. The luck went our way that night. We were two up early on."

"I though both penalties were quite fair. And then Robin got that tremendous goal", I added.

"I don't remember the goal. I remember the two penalties because Tranmere were great promotion rivals and we got a great start on them. I thought one of them wasn't a penalty for sure. It won the match for us, it was over then."

But the party spirit and exuberance went right through to the final whistle. It's the part of the game supporters often enjoy and remember most. As far as we're concerned, the job isn't finished when you're 2-0 up. That's when the entertainment should start. That night we weren't disappointed as we so often are when teams spend the last half hour saving their energy for the next match.

Even without the aid of television cameras the memory of Robin's curling volley has, in the way of Banks's save, become sanctified and preserved for those who saw it. It was even recalled in his recent obituary.

Such incidents get into the collective memory by repetition, discussion, embroidery and more repetition. They gain strength and vitality and become the unquestionable icons we want them to become. But nowadays television is their life force. Without it they can fade and die.

Was Banks's save really that good? He had time to get over to the other side of the goal while the ball was in the air. I'm sure I've seen Steve Death make a better save from a worse position but, as Fred Binney of Exeter City isn't quite the totemic foe that is Pele of Brazil, and there are no pictures or fellow communicants to back me, that achievement has withered to nothing in the stock of our collective reminiscences.

It is simpler to trust the agreed verdict of generations. And it troubles me a little that Eamon didn't recall the moment that came to symbolise the winning of promotion for the first time in half a century.

There followed a 0-0 draw at Rochdale in front of barely a thousand people and a vital 1-0 win at Bournemouth. Huddersfield made two draws; Tranmere won, then lost at home.

With five to play Reading had three points over Tranmere and four over Huddersfield who, as ever, had a game in hand. Though it was looking good the next two games were against Lincoln and Northampton, respectively nine and five points ahead of Reading.

MOSS, FOSTER, HOWELLS, SEDUNARY AND BROOKS

EVENING POST, 10 APRIL 1976

Traditionally there has been an element of THEM and US in the club-supporter relationship. It dates from the "bad old days" when clubs were rich and supporters were simply something that made turnstiles click.

Those days are over, a fact that has penetrated all but the thickest football skull and now most successful soccer teams boast an active, capably run supporters club.

Alas, because the spotlight is focused on the playing side of a club, the efforts of those actively engaged behind the scenes tend to go unnoticed. Yet it is no exaggeration to say that without such people many League clubs would cease to exist.

Much is written about our success on the field this season, but it is worth pointing out that what we have achieved has been matched and indeed surpassed by the achievements of the supporters club.

BATTLED

Whilst we have battled to shed our Fourth Division rags, the supporters club, led by Jim Brooks and Albert Moss, can claim riches of which many Second Division clubs would be proud. In a very real sense the activites of the supporters club have laid the foundation for our success on the field.

And although the dedicated army who assist Jim and Albert won't be doing a lap of honour when we go up, their contribution should not go unrecognised.

Whilst Friday, Cumming, Hiron and Murray are names with which we are all familiar, those of Moss, Foster, Howells and Sedunary are less known; yet the commitment of such men is just as crucial to our success.

The figures allow no one to doubt otherwise.

Last season the club made a profit of £19,000 which was exactly the sum contributed by the supporters club. Each week 32,000 bingo tickets are sold by an army of agents. Men like Harry Smith and Pip Attwell.

This year Jim Brooks is confident that the record £25,000 contribution of two years ago will be broken, money that ultimately will enable the wages to be paid or players to be bought.

That kind of money represents the devotion and spare

time of many dedicated people. Their commitment is to Reading Football Club and no one has greater claims to a share of the glory than them.

Typically, men like Moss and Brooks seek not so much the glory as the opportunity to use our present success on the field as a means of extending their activities.

They talk urgently of the task of attracting more gents to sell bingo tickets, of imaginative social evenings to be put on at the supporters club.

It means more hard work, more chunks of free time sacrificed as they strive to develop an even more successful club.

RUTHLESS

This has been the most satisfying week of the season despite a rather painful start at Rochdale. We never really played and although various excuses could be advanced - reaction to the Tranmere game, depression due to the dismal atmosphere, etc., etc., - none are really acceptable.

Still, Tuesday's result from Tranmere gave us a big incentive to get something at Bournemouth. I seem to spend half my life waiting for Angela Rippon to read the football results and for a change the news was good.

Bournemouth was even better. We produced our best away performance of the season against a decent young side for whom this was a last chance to revive promotion hopes.

Dennis Nelson got the winner - a typically ruthless piece of finishing. He will be my first pick in five-a-side from now on. There's no higher praise.

So with five to go things look good and one senses that even the direst cynics are beginning to relent. Not that people who went to Bournemouth come into that category. They were magnificent, their support was heard and appreciated.

Dougie Webb, an old adversary, travelled with us to Bournemouth and it was good to see him again.

I remember a particularly bruising encounter at Elm Park when Dougie played for Reading and I for a Millwall side that went on to gain promotion.

"Dougie" is now in charge of the club's successful youth scheme, looking fit and well; in fact living proof that there is hope for us old pros yet.

None of the playing staff of Dunphy's era is still at the club, (though local boy Dougie Webb did his bit for the club, fathering young Neil - sold, alas, to Portsmouth before he was even fully grown).

Of the supporters mentioned in this column, one became a director of the club, another an employee, while others still carry on as volunteers today.

"Players come to respect these people more at the end of their careers. In an emotional sense it's their club," says Eamon, "not the players' or the directors'."

Some of the players became fans themselves again. Plenty would have been after tickets for the match against Lincoln City, already - with seven games to play - assured of promotion. The largest crowd of the season, 15,683, was present.

For the first time ever a Reading match had a sponsor - "My Goodness Stores" (the place to shoot straight in to for fruit and vegetables). I've even kept their bloody hand bill inside the programme as if, touched by the magic of the occasion, it might acquire some official or mythic value!

The big game ended in a rather anti-climactic 1-1 draw. Lincoln did look good but not that good. The second half was flat rather than the hammer and tongs we'd expected. A week later, on Good Friday, Reading were unluckily slaughtered 4-1 at Northampton, having had an obvious penalty turned down when one up.

The vulnerability of the defence to a higher class of football was clear - and we still needed three points to reach that higher class. Huddersfield had, at last, won for the first time in eight games.

WE DON'T TAKE EACH GAME AS IT COMES

EVENING POST, 17 APRIL 1976

Just seven days and three games to go.

If I talk about a "moment of truth" you may well accuse me of being melodramatic. Yet for us at Elm Park, and for all those in contention for the season's prizes the drama of the next week is very real.

The prize we have spent months, perhaps years, working for, dreaming about, is now within our grasp and the prospect is at once exhilarating and a little frightening.

Joy at having almost reached the summit is mixed with anxiety at the thought that a bad week now could see you tumbling back down to obscurity.

It doesn't really matter whether what you seek is promotion from Division Four or the First Division Championship - the figures are different, the emotions just the same.

Not surprisingly one feels, at this stage, one's whole existence revolving around football and the task in hand, your thoughts constantly invaded by the speculative bug.

SPECULATING

Departing Prime Ministers, the falling pound, mother-in-law's rheumatism and our moulting cat, matters great and small, fail to move you now.

Your head is full in thinking of the next game, of what it will be like to win and of what awaits you if you lose.

You project yourself on to summer and wonder what it will be like. Will you spend it contented, at peace with yourself, reflecting on your success? Or miserable, consumed by regret at an opportunity missed?

Speculating thus, the pressures mount as you realise how much it means to be successful. And as recent results show, those pressures take their toll. Palace, Tranmere, Brighton, Bolton, Huddersfield, West Brom, all victims of their own anxiety, falling now to sides they would have beaten a few weeks ago.

Wisdom in this situation is represented by those who deny the speculative bug and confine themselves to the task of winning the next game.

In a brave attempt to project an image of cool composure pros are often quoted as follows "We are not getting carried away. We are taking one game at a time and are not concerned with what the other contenders do."

THEORY

In theory it sounds good, in practice it's never quite as they say.

I once dismissed a journalist with just such a phrase, only to find myself half an hour later in advanced mathematics working out what might happen three games on.

Of course the truth is that like everyone else the pro indulges in a degree of speculation, but being more familiar with the game's capacity for springing surprises he places less faith in his calculations.

In fact, at this stage in the season, results are impossible to predict simply because the atmosphere in which they are played is so unreal.

So although you ought to beat X and your rivals might be expected to struggle against Y it very often turns out the opposite - if you see what I mean.

You can give yourself a headache working out the various permutations and in the end it all boils down to getting your own results right.

To do that we need to keep our heads, forget the past, postpone the future, and focus on our next opponents.

The most important news of the week has nothing to do with promotion (important that is for those not concerned in promotion).

Arsenal, in a bold, imaginative move, announced their desire to have Real Madrid's Yugoslav manager as successor to Bertie Mee. A marriage between one of the world's leading coaches and the Arsenal is a fascinating prospect, but Real are not keen to part.

Is our traditional insularity to be discarded? How would Miljanic approach the unique problems posed by the English League season?

Miljanic is on record as being a passionate advocate of attacking, entertaining football.

"I don't want to win European Cups, or even World Cups unless my team plays genuine entertaining football. We have to play with enthusiasm and freedom, with attack as the main objective."

Can such brave sentiments be reconciled with the 60 game season, with conditions that range from ice to mud, with players less technically gifted than their European counterparts?

For a game starved of original ideas in which too many idealists have been defeated by reality the arrival of a coach of Miljanic's stature would be very good news.

Well, it only took another fifteen years before Aston Villa actually took the plunge and appointed the Czech national manager Josef Venglos - and let him go a year later.

Back on Good Friday afternoon 1976, Tranmere did themselves, and Reading, a favour by stuffing Huddersfield 3-0.

When the end comes, it comes in rushing. Easter Monday, Reading against old rivals Brentford here to spoil and nick a point. Huddersfield at home to hapless Southport.

Twenty minutes to go at Elm Park, 12,000 tempers frayed, Robin Friday, battered black and blue already, on the ball again, past one and another, corkscrewing into the box, against the bloody post. Old man Hiron's there, on the rebound, back of the net, 1-0, goodnight Brentford. And news from Huddersfield on the radio. Incredibly they're down 2-1 with a knot of marooned Reading supporters cheering Southport on. Hara-kiri at Huddersfield, joy at Elm Park.

We need one point from two games. Did those pre-war nearly men of Division Three South ever come this close and blow it? Who knows or, at this moment, cares...

Two days later a midweek game at Cambridge, with over a thousand Reading fans in a crowd of 3,245. We absolutely had to be there because this could be the decisive one. At last Reading were in the full glare of the promotion spotlight. Cambridge were a coming side, destined to be champions next season. Gordon Cumming was back in for John Murray. It was a specific game, that Eamon Dunphy did remember.

"Ron Atkinson was their manager. We played well but had to hold on desperately because our nerves had gone. I remember Atkinson afterwards, he was a very good sport".

Friday gave Reading the lead in the first minute. Steve Spriggs equalised and the unlikely combination of Bryan Carnaby's right boot and a bump in the pitch gave Reading the goal that ultimately secured promotion. Cambridge threw everything forward in the second half, got another equaliser, had Brendan Batson sent off for a ruck with Friday and still kept pouring forward. Geoff Barker came on for Eamon Dunphy and that bald pate helped keep the ten men out. Now it was absolutely necessary to sing and we did. The ground rang with encouragement for Reading. It had been so long, it was now so close and it still looked bloody precarious. Promotion, after all, was still something other teams did. Then time - and Reading - were up. Across the pitch, into the stand, cheering, singing and grasping for the players' jerseys.

For ten minutes or so there was absolute exhilaration. All the world's a friend etc., etc. The police had locked us in the ground 'for our own safety' so we carried on stomping on the seats and celebrating in song.

Because two of us were staying the night with a friend

in Cambridge we were OK for a pint or two afterwards. Others, sadly, were not so fortunate which is a bit of a dampener.

The next day was full of acknowledgements from friends who supported teams like Leeds and Liverpool. If a fellow has to support Reading, they reasoned, it's only fair he should be happy once in a while. On my part, there was relief at the success. Publicly bearing your support for an unfashionable team that fails, brings you mock sympathy and misplaced scorn. You feel like saying it's not me that's got the problem, it's the team. I was just born that way. I can't be helped. But not today, today was fine.

Each of us, of course, has our own particular perspective on that moment.

REDEMPTION

EVENING POST, 24 APRIL 1976

Moments of pure joy. Feelings beyond the reach of the richest mortal. A sense of achievement, of pride and of simple, rarely felt, happiness. The first moments of realisation, that beautiful weightless feeling as the fear and tension of the past few weeks seeps away.

We're up. We've done it . Head full of crazy thoughts. The failures of the past, of efforts unrewarded, of wounds from lost campaigns, of long remembered indignities. All now erased.

You've proved yourself, succeeded where you might have failed and now in these moments you stand flawless, supreme, at peace.

If you're a Fourth Division player these moments are sweet indeed.

The Fourth Division - football's knackers yard - so they say. A place for "has beens" and "never will bes". We've been there, feelings of rejection, inadequacy, of failure. Somewhere in the past a manager has told you you're not good enough, stripped you of your pride.

To hell with him now. You've overturned his verdict, won your own justice, retrieved your self-respect.

Outwardly you have had to live with that assessment of your worth. But in your heart you never did and this triumph is your vindication.

The Fourth Division - a knackers yard? Not really. There are many honest pros, and some talented youngsters amongst them, who lack only the good fortune to play for Reading, Lincoln, instead of Southport, Rochdale, etc.

Twelve months ago I sat in Lewisham Hospital and with heavy heart listened to an orthopaedic specialist advise me to quit the game. I'd suffered severe back pains for two years and despite the probings of an army of specialists the cause remained unknown.

Finally I had a gland removed for tests, an event that had fairly sinister undertones but which fortunately left me in the clear.

So they diagnosed wear and tear. Fifteen years spent dragging my puny nine stone around the Football League was at last taking its toll "I'm very sorry, Mr Dunphy", the dreaded words. I went home to cry.

It was promotion year at Charlton. I'd played 20 odd games, including three of the last four, but I was dropped for the final game, and in general left alone to my problems.

I was, quite simply, eminently dispensable and when the season ended I was given a free transfer.

There was more than a hint that my back trouble was "in the mind" and only became acute when I wasn't playing well.

I sat at home confused and bitter. Was I finished? Was the trouble in my head? Who could tell? Who bloody cared?

Me. So, one last throw of the dice, I went to an acupuncture clinic. The atmosphere there was amazingly positive in contrast to the air of weary cynicism I'd encountered in more orthodox establishments.

And the treatment gave me relief. I could go on playing. The question was - could I find a club? Who was in the market for an ageing midfield player with a suspect back?

Soon the offers were trickling in. The Wagga Wagga Teetotalling Club in the Australian Outback were very interested. The game out there was "developing fast" and they'd fix me up with a job. How about a new life in New Zealand? Sheep Farmers Celtic required an "experienced player", could I please send details?

Desperation was setting in. Social Security beckoning. And then an English voice on the phone. Not Don Revie, but Alan Batsford, manager of Wimbledon, and I was very grateful. At least they were the best Southern League club and although six months ago I would have scorned their approach, now I was gratified by it.

We talked terms. He was ambitious, impressive, but I was still reluctant. There must be a League club somewhere?

Some weeks previously I'd phoned Charlie Hurley, my only personal approach. He'd been interested a couple of years ago. I wondered if perhaps?... I'd heard nothing since, almost certainly wouldn't. He seemed non-committal. "I'll give you a ring". Oh yeah.

No, it looked like Wimbledon or Beachy Head.

The day before I was due to sign Charlie Hurley called back. "Are you fixed up yet?" "Well". I stalled, trying to conceal the excitement, "I've got a few irons in the fire", (my bloody head in the oven more like). "Why don't you come down and have a chat," said he.

"I suppose I could" (suppose I could!).

Next day terms were quickly agreed. They didn't ask for much! Wagga Wagga, Sheep Farmers Celtic and the Southern League postponed for another year.

I remember those days, the memory strong within me now. The other lads have, doubtless, similar tales to tell. Now at this moment those wounds are healed.

If nothing else a life spent in this game ought to bestow on one a modicum of humility. Success is very often a matter of good fortune.

Being in a certain place at the right time, working for and with good people, pooling your talents, however modest, with your fellow pros. Football and good football clubs rely on teamwork - a cliche, perhaps, but it's absolutely true.

This week the limelight focuses on the eleven players fortunate enough to be at this moment in the first team; that is unfortunate and misleading.

Points won early in the season count equally with those latterly gained, but for a variety of reasons guys who earned them now find themselves in the stands.

By a quirk of fate it could be anyone of us sitting it out. We've all had our share, and will again in this game of ups and downs.

Right now for lads like Bruce Stuckey and Steve Death the feeling is bitter sweet. It takes an effort of mind to remember the games Death saved, Southport home and away. Bruce's magic on the left wing.

Memories can be incredibly short in this game, especially in the glory days. One of the nicest aspects of our success is the fact that everyone has been a part of it; it isn't always so.

Finally the relief at bidding farewell to the "50-year-old hoodoo" that has hung over this club. It was an inheritance any team could have done without.

At least we have dispelled a myth that, in the sense of the pressure it created, had become a reality.

No more of that "Reading will never do it" nonsense. The teams of the future should be grateful for that.

One last profound pleasure. Seeing the faces of people who've supported and believed in this club for years. The kind of people whose loyalty and devotion give football its point. The people I see in the supporters club before games, and standing in the freezing rain at Workington, Rochdale and other exotic stops along the way.

The guy with the sandwiches, well spoken, smiling, pleasant always, no matter how grim the debacle.

The man who travels with his sons, "Reading forever" who writes me letters and cheers me up, who even forgave us Huddersfield.

The pretty girl who wears the Eamonn Dunphy badge, but replaces it with Gary Peters when I have a "stinker".

And others, so many other incredible people, who mean so much to us and to the game. Happy now. We're all happy now.

Looking back fifteen years later Eamon smiled ruefully. There was a great deal of truth and insight in that column.

"A lot of players in the Third and Fourth Divisions were not fulfilled at that level. They were badly affected by the situation they found themselves in. It was really poignant. They were not very confident as players though they might be as people. But the past is always there to haunt you. When you get success there's a terrific redemption of all the past failures in your football life and it can lead to a whole new chapter in your career."

Redemption, then, for the players and a belief that progress was possible for the club. The hoodoo was gone and the teams of the future should indeed be grateful to this side. Promotion from the Fourth was achieved again in 1979 and 1984 and from the Third in 1986 without much sense of a historical burden. Indeed, every subsequent serious promotion challenge has ended in success.

A crowd of 12,229 gathered to acclaim the promoted heroes before the game against Crewe Alexandra. Reading won easily, 3-1, with Dunphy scoring his third goal of the season from close range.

FINAL TABLE - DIVISION FOUR

	P	W	D	L	W	D	L	F	A	PTS
1. Lincoln City	46	21	2	0	11	8	4	111	39	74
2. Northampton T	46	18	5	0	11	5	7	87	40	68
3. Reading	46	19	3	1	5	9	9	70	51	60
4. Tranmere R	46	18	3	2	6	7	10	89	55	58
5. Huddersfield T	46	11	6	6	10	8	5	56	41	56

OF FLAT CHAMPAGNE, UNBURNT TOAST & TENDER BEEF

EVENING POST, 1 MAY 1976

After three days celebration reaction is setting in. The bubbles have gone flat and I'm my old, manic depressive, self again. As Robin, a fellow MD remarked in a quiet moment yesterday: "The feeling doesn't last long does it."

'The feeling' - pleasant three pint drunkenness - could, over the past three days, be achieved without alcoholic assistance: today I think I would need the three pints!

Inevitably, our descent from the euphoric heights is causing 're-entry' problems. The most immediate being Crewe. On the face of it the stage is set for an afternoon of celebration. Big crowd, eager to acclaim, mediocre opposition, a sacrificial offering at the altar of our success, no pressure ... the perfect script.

Sadly, the game is an anti-climax. Emotions drained, bodies tired, high wind, bumpy pitch, honest, hustling opponents. Crowd impatient, anxious not to be denied their celebration. A struggle. Managing, just, to keep our head in front. An imperfect end to a perfect season.

CHAMPAGNE

Afterwards take a bow, drink some more champagne, accept congratulations, another outstretched hand, another happy face.

Talk briefly to Warwick Rimmer, veteran Crewe defender. "Well done lad." A pro's greeting. Warwick... I've seen him around for a decade. Honest, working as hard today as he ever did. Bolton was his club. Solid, reliable. He's enjoyed it. We talk a little of the Fourth Division horrors. Workington, Southport, thin crowds, small material reward.

He smiles wryly, contemplating next season. I silently rejoice in my good fortune.

SUNDAY: "The feeling" may have gone but a profound sense of satisfaction remains.

This morning I receive the ultimate promotion prize - breakfast in bed - and as a special treat my wife hasn't burnt the toast!

MONDAY: A trip to the cattle market where keen supporter Mr Stevens is bidding for a bullock which he is to present to us as thank-you for promotion.

AUCTION

Our fellow, weighing 8 1/2 hundredweight, is noosed and led into the auction ring. He casts a baleful eye in our direction, which we shiftily manage to avoid.

Bidding is brisk before Mr Stevens secures the victim of our success. Farming friends assure me that cows are dumb, but this fellow obviously knew that something was up.

As we compassionately calculated how many pounds of beef we'd cop he was dragged reluctantly towards the slaughterhouse, but not before he'd had his photo taken with his newly acquired "friends". We patted him reassuringly and hoped the meat would be tender!

As the poor sod departed to his fate I couldn't help but consider that had the results gone differently we might have been treading the same path!

TUESDAY: Now I know how the bullock felt. 0-4 to Coventry City, a result that pleased nobody, least of all the boss. He gave us hell, justifiably.

As I have said here before, friendly games against First Division opponents are difficult for other than obvious reasons. The gap in skill can only be bridged by a massive effort and a degree of physical contact. In other words you ought to get "stuck in".

But in a friendly game this isn't really on. So you lay off, allow them to display their skills, and get stuffed. Lacking concentration and a competitive edge we never had a chance. The plea is guilty.

The vexed question of cup final tickets. I sent mine to my Dad! He was giving it to a friend at work who does him occasional favours. A trickle of graft that develops into an ocean of corruption?

Should I, and 50,000 others with no obvious claims, be offered the chance to buy tickets when thousands of Manchester and Saints fans miss out?

Those subjected to my greedily anxious inquiries - "where's my ticket" - may raise an eyebrow now, nevertheless I ask the question more or less sincerely. One thing that is clear is that too many of the 50,000 "spare" tickets end up in the grasping hands of the "touts".

MYSTERY

Of course a fair proportion of those come from players despite a system that allows the FA to identify the the original owner.

Why the law cannot proceed against the "touts" who operate outside the stadium remains shrouded in legal mystery. Common sense it seems has no place in law.

Of course there are some who wouldn't want to go to Wembley even if guaranteed a seat in the Royal Box. Me for one.

Rightly or wrongly Cup Final has for me become a TV occasion. In fact it's always been so.

As a small boy I used to cross Dublin to see the final on my aunt's flickering nine-inch screen. The heavenly excitement of the day accentuated by the fear that Aunt Carmel's telly would pack up at a crucial moment.

Days of Kenneth Wolstenholme, heroic Bert Trautman, tragic Roy Dwight and fated Man United.

GUEST

I was an apprentice pro at Man United in 1963, when they played Leicester in the final. There, as a guest, within hailing distance of the Royal Box, I remember best being moved by the hymn Abide With Me.

Looking back now I'd still swop my stand seat for the magic of my aunt's sitting room and thus it remains to this day.

With Wolstenholme gone, Coleman is my hero now. He transports me to the team's hotel, the coach en route to the stadium, the twin towered view down Wembley Way at half-past one.

Out on to the pitch before the game with Barry Davies, pre-match comments and half-time analysis from Don Revie and the panel.

And afterwards the action replay of the winning goal, the hero of the hour "Talking us through it", the player splashing happily in the bath and Coleman, a nerve tingling six hour stint behind him, as composed and banal as ever.

Cup Final day by the TV, a priceless experience not to be traded for a place among the sweaty, thirsty, travel weary, comfortless, 100,000 unlucky enough to have a ticket.

Feet up, lager at fingertips, wife in kitchen making sandwiches (burnt!) who could ask for anything more.

THURSDAY: A very special night out. We've been saving up all season for a "players celebration" and tonight's the night.

Maybe the real triumph, in the end, does belong to the fans even if all we do is invade the pitch and go home for tea. The sharing-out of that carcass in the close season is a completely co-incidental yet powerful metaphor of what Eamon felt had happened to his team-mates. They'd won, they'd had some laughs and terrors on the way and, in the end, they felt they had been sold down the river and split up. The fans, if they bothered, would keep the memories. It'll be better than the brisket in fifteen years time for sure.

"There's something very transient about the life of a professional footballer. You live for the moment, take the moment and look for where you get the next one. It's survival and you don't have time to savour or treasure... the reality of a pro footballer, as the experience at Reading shows, was within days of getting promotion and achieving a bit of history for the town we were outcasts, renegades and on the way out. The best thing that could have happened to us that year was to miss promotion by a couple of points. We'd have earned much more money the next year, we'd have been successful and we'd have gone on to play another two or three years. So by the very fact of winning promotion we'd dug our own graves. In that kind of environment you tend to forget about the future and not worry about it."

A sanguine and frightening view that corresponds with the old joke about the manager encouraging his side to win a cup-tie so he'd be able to afford to buy players to replace them with. Great for the fans but ......

Many of the serious matters that happen in a football club take place during the close season. While 'Charlie Hurley's blue and white army' sweltered in the original 'phew what a scorcher' summer, Reading Football Club imploded.

As Hurley was looking for two or three more players his squad met, enraged over a pint of lager and a bag of brisket, in the Spread Eagle, the pub at the corner of the ground. At first none of them would take the terms the club had offered for the next season. Youlden asked to go on the transfer list. Then, at the end of July, Geoff Barker dramatically quit the game altogether. The former Darlington and Hull City centre-half became a symbolic figure for Eamon and the column he wrote about Geoff's predicament was the one of which he was most proud and most clearly remembers today.

ALL TO BE A BLOODY SALES REP.

EVENING POST, 24 JULY 1976

Geoff Barker has played his last game of League football. Unable to agree terms for a new contract he has, at the age of 27, quit the game to take a job as a sales rep. This is not the place to argue the merit of his claim. That is a personal matter best debated elsewhere and I don't propose to put my spoke in.

But what I feel should be put on record is my professional respect and personal affection for Geoff. There are two good reasons for doing so. Firstly because my feelings for Geoff are widely shared at the club, and secondly because too often blokes like Geoff drift quietly out of football, their deeds unrecorded, their passing unmourned.

Geoff was not a star, indeed it is ironic that probably the biggest headline he ever made was the one announcing his departure. Yet he was an important figure in the game, for the values he embodied were those of the average pro, the sort that good clubs are founded on.

Dedication, honesty, a sense of responsibility, to his colleagues, to the club, and a love of the game that enables one to cope with and actually enjoy its ups and downs. If you hired Geoff Barker you were getting plenty for your money.

He cared about the game and about his part in it. He never missed training, always did his best when he was there. He rarely seemed to be ill, always showed up. Geoff was dependable, and, it seems, expendable.

To really understand the importance of Geoff it was necessary to spend Saturday afternoon in his company. Better still, a cold, wet, northern, winter Saturday with the mud and the boots flying. The kind of day when inspiration is badly needed and there's no home crowd to provide it.

On such occasions - and in Division Four they are depressingly numerous - Geoff was the source of inspiration. Time after time that old bald head would rise to thump danger away.

CUNNING

He wouldn't duck his responsibility and watching him you wouldn't be inclined to either. He was a good man in a crisis and away from home last season we had a few of those.

His particular qualities were less obvious in home games where more often than not glory is the name of the game. But he did have one outstanding moment at Elm Park last season.

It came in the tight promotion battle against Northampton when the score was 0-0 and we desperately needed a break. Suddenly up popped Geoff with a glorious close-in volley which settled the game in our favour. A rare moment of glory.

Equally scarce were Geoff's stinkers, but he like the rest of us had them. One in particular stands out. It was at Barnsley where a cunning little centre-forward gave Geoff the biggest chasing of his life.

The guy went to town, scoring a couple, laying one on, and in general giving a passable impression of Geoff Hurst. If ever a situation called for some judicious violence this was it, but far from kicking the bloke Geoff couldn't get near enough to shoot him.

We eventually lost 4-2 and Geoff took plenty of stick in the dressing room afterwards. But he took it like a man. He was hurt, but determined too.

It would be a while before it happened again, and it was. We went to Newport on the Monday night where a 0-0 draw restored our pride and Geoff's peace of mind. Thus the life of the average pro. His disaster on Saturday makes headlines, his competence on Monday is taken for granted.

A dash of glory here, a small disaster there, but mainly sheer, unspectacular, honesty. Not necessarily the stuff that stars are made of, but rather what good pros depend on. And on the whole, it is good pros rather than stars that make a good club.

IRONIC

Now for Geoff Barker, good lad, good player, good pro, the game must taste a trifle bitter. It is sadly ironic that he should now find himself out of the game. Having seen his labours bear fruit, for the only time in his career, he finds himself excluded from the feast. All must seem in vain. The dedication, the caring, the small defeats, the great victories, what does it matter to him now?

Is this what he - and we - sweated blood to achieve? Did he do it all to become a bloody sales rep?

Geoff leaves football with nothing more than our respect and affection. He takes his leave as he entered - quietly.

His passing goes unnoticed, remains unmourned. It doesn't really matter because there are other lads like Geoff who will do a similar kind of job. In our wonderful game the dependables are expendable. That at least is how the cynics, the "realists" see it. Others, more romantic, wonder about the future.

Be lucky Geoff.

"Everyone at the club knew what that column meant", said Eamon, looking back, "It caused me a lot of problems with them."

"Geoff was the archetypal lower division footballer who was shat on and he just had no defence against it at all. The arguments weren't about vast sums of money. They were about principles. The thing that threw Geoff out of the game was partly money but largely not being appreciated and valued the way he ought to have been."

"They were a bad lot of people running Reading Football Club then. They were living in the 1940's and 1950's. They were a club that never had to change, and that's why they had never had any success. It was the very people that brought that success to them that irritated them most."

"Geoff was on £50 per week. His family were in dire straits. Other guys were getting bad money too. It was shabby, wrong treatment. In the 1970's everyone was insulated from the pressure of life by benefits - unlike some professional sportsmen who had very little."

"You'd be on the terraces slagging off this guy who had nothing anyway. It was a ridiculous situation where guys were local heroes but the reality was that their lives were shit, they were living hand-to-mouth. I was uncomfortable and angry about it at the time so I was writing from that perspective. Trying to tell the reader of the Evening Post that this is what it's like and the notion you have of it is quite false."

"To me Geoff's a noble and heroic figure who stands in stark contrast to the Frank Wallers of this world," (n.b. Waller was the Chairman who later sold his stake in the club to Robert Maxwell as part of the "Thames Valley Royals" deal). "He's the guy I was really interested in. I don't think supporters really understand guys like Geoff, supporters are really condescending to a fellow like that, they jeer him, bye, bye old Geoff. They don't feel it the way a pro feels it. They don't know it, they couldn't expect to feel it."

I had, still have of course, a Geoff Barker badge. I admit it was a condescending and ironic 'bad taste' statement on my part. At least the club didn't leave him out when the badges were made.

Seriously though, Eamon is, alas, right. We don't know it, we can't expect to feel it. For me, Geoff was just an average stopper. His game never rose to the heights where you'd expect him to be a major influence on the outcome. More likely a bigger bloke would outjump him and a faster bloke outrun him and there would be plenty more of those around in the Third Division.

Of course one has human sympathy for someone doing his best but, as a fan, you're only really interested in the relative worth of that "best", his playing capability. If that isn't there, there's no basis for further long term goodwill. As fans we want to see people play much better than we think we can ourselves. If he can't it's just another shirt awaiting a fresh occupant. It actually only takes three or four games to make your mind up. With the burden of our dreams and expectations there isn't much sentiment on the supporters' side of the fence either.

But in no sense could this argument condone the club's treatment in general of its playing staff. What went on in July and August was more important, in retrospect, that any of the 46 matches that were to follow.

Four days after that column appeared Robin Friday asked for a transfer. "There doesn't seem to be any ambition at the club," he said. "If you ask me they'd be happy enough to stroll on in the bottom half of the Third Division forever." A week later John Murray joined Youlden and Friday on the list. Cumming, Death and Dunphy contined to refuse terms until it was pointed out that a new PFA regulation meant that if no new deal was signed by August 12 a player would have to continue on last year's terms. Cumming and Dunphy signed.

On the opening day of the League season, with Turner injured, Death, still unsigned, refused to play and the team coach left without him. A local journalist persuaded Death out of bed and took him to Gillingham in his car. Deathie had a blinder.

Earlier in the day, following yet more ructions between Hurley and himself during a League Cup tie, Eamon Dunphy was given a free transfer.

"Once you've been shabbily treated by a club it breaks that nebulous camaraderie that sustained you in tough games, or when you go behind. It becomes impossible to be successful then."

The implication of that view is that you don't try as hard as you might have done. Forty six League games later, Reading were relegated back to Division Four.

PART THREE

ARE WE IN THIS TOGETHER?

Addiction, obligation and separate worlds

There is much in the preceding pages about the player's and fan's different perspectives on the same objectives and events.

Before considering the wider aspects of the player - fan relationship, let's deal briefly with Reading's 1975/76 promotion season and that great old question, "What does it mean to you?"

From a vantage point of fifteen years if you, as fan, can retain three or four pleasant, positive memories from a season's watching, you'll be doing well. 1975/76 was certainly among the better years of supporting Reading FC. Some subsequent seasons have incurred almost total mental wipe-out!

For Eamon Dunphy, an integral part of the team that made it happen it, alas, doesn't matter a bean now.

"What I feel for Reading is nothing. It was something I did that worked for the club for a period of time. In the end it didn't work for me or most of the other guys. I don't feel bitter about it, just cold."

"I've only been back to Reading twice, to the Crown Court where someone I knew was on trial. It's a most peculiar town. I felt it had no soul. Most people who live there don't come from Reading. I hated it. I used to race to the station, didn't hang around at all. Other places I'd been in, South London, Manchester, had a certain richness. Reading was like the Betjeman view of Slough."

I don't know what it is about our quite pleasant market town (and thriving regional centre) that continually attracts such criticism. Perhaps it is the lack of obvious defects and salient characteristics. Maybe to the world at large Reading is no more than a glorified crossroads signposting more recognisable attractions, a place people pass through without ever feeling they belong. Perhaps it's vilified merely because it defies typecasting in a single glib phrase or image. Still, we're stoical about it. We have our own richness too. And everywhere is home for someone. Reading just happens to be it for me.

"There was no close relationship between the player and the town. I feel nothing at all for Reading and nothing for Millwall now either."

Yet despite these feelings, and a general antipathy towards the Football League and its clubs, Eamon is still well-informed about the major events at Elm Park in the years since he left. But his interest would not extend to visiting Elm Park.

"I wouldn't want to go. You couldn't twist my arm. Not even out of curiosity. I'd find it very sad. You don't want to see something you love (football) in its desecrated state."

Supporters don't see things in quite such black and white terms - but they are the ones who are still going! Though many of my friends no longer go and I don't enjoy it or look forward to it as much, I'm still there, still gutted if we lose a local derby. I agree with Eamon, it is getting harder to play football in a way that is as attractive to spectators. Through improved fitness and tactics players seem to cover more ground and leave less space to play in. They seem much more to be slaves of the manager's bidding, not free to express themselves either on or off the pitch. As a columnist, as well as passing midfielder, Dunphy has had notably few successors.

For Eamon the best relationship he had with the supporters of Reading was through the back page of the Evening Post. Even so, it had its limitations as this final extract from 31 July 1976 shows.

Regular readers of this column (I hope you're both well) will be well aware of my craving need to attack the "ghosts" and may well suspect me of doing so with the sole objective of establishing my own credentials. What nasty, malicious minds my regular readers have. Nothing, of course, could be further from the truth.

No, the point of all this is that in the circumstances in which I find myself on this Saturday morning I am feeling in need of a few well worn cliches.

You see it has been a lousy week. My big toe has prevented me from doing any real training and the wage negotiations that have dragged on all summer are consuming time and energy that might otherwise be usefully spent in pursuit of fitness.

Or as a clever "ghost" might put it, the injury is taking a little longer than expected and although I've not yet signed a new contract I'm sure the problems will soon be ironed out.

It is all very well writing a column like this when things are going well, it is when things are slightly less than ideal that the problems begin.

Thus this morning is spent attempting to steer a course between (A) being in breach of contract (I am forbidden to discuss club business in the Press - unfavourable business that is): (B) the dreaded "the lads are rarin' to go".

In the end I decide to postpone a decision on the grounds that I'm getting a headache and anyway this could

*be my last Saturday morning in bed for ten months (unless
I choose course A).*

It is obviously difficult to write openly about a job whilst
you are actually doing it because of the effect it has on
others. But Dunphy does enough to strip professional
football of its deceptive glamour so we can understand the
dynamics and workings behind the stardom and the cliche.

At times the way he portrays his professional life makes
it seem like working on a building-site. I put the comparison
to Eamon:

"Your view of the world as a player is completely
internalised. You've got a gaffer, a set of mates and a task
to do. You don't give a toss one way or another about who
is actually in the building when you've built it. You get some
money and you have a row if someone else is doing the
same thing and getting more. You move on and forget the
building."

"That's a fair sort of comparison," he replied, " except
the difference between a building site and a football team is
that there are spectators and that if you don't do your job
you won't get your fucking money. There's a penalty clause,
that's the difference, that's the discipline that doesn't exist
elsewhere. And if the discipline of the professional footballer
was inflicted on every walk of life then society would
function differently and better than it does now."

So, though the fans are outside the world of the
professional footballer, they act both as potential penalty
clause and occasional encouragement. "Fans are important
to it but you're not actually doing it for them", concludes
Dunphy.

This makes us sound like final, but distant, arbiters
whose criticisms, however unjust to the player's view, do
actually play an active part in the whole shooting match. If it
is true, it takes an awful lot of shouting to get heard.

How does the role, the commitment, addiction even, of
the fan affect the player? What obligations does it impose
on him?

Football is unique among major British club sports in
freely publishing its crowd figures. On that very simple,
factual level the role of the crowd is acknowledged.

Many people are defined by their allegiance to a
particular team. To describe someone as 'a big Arsenal fan'
does not, necessarily, suggest he is a gross human being;
rather, that a large portion of his life is devoted to following
the Arsenal.

Not all fans fit into this pattern. Some go to a football
match in much the same way as they might go to a circus -
for the pleasure of a shared spectacle. Others go as a

matter of social routine and a few even go to cause trouble. But the bedrock of a club's support is that proportion who religiously attend almost each and every home game. Within this there are the most loyal of loyal fans, numbering about a coachload in the lower divisions, who are beyond rational thought and travel to all the forlorn midweek defeats hundreds of miles away.

If Geoff Barker was the man (or symbol) Eamon Dunphy was really interested in then these are people who I most feel for. They are addicts. Sometimes they have to support the club despite the current team and regime. They exist in a completely unbalanced relationship, committed to something over which they have no control and about which they are often kept in the dark. As a small huddle on a distant rainswept terrace or in the early hours of a motorway service station morning they seek, unconsciously, to "act" as the moral penalty clause to the players lest they forget their obligations to the town and the people who pay their wages.

The manager and players are guardians of that trust and blind loyalty. They are always expected to deliver or play to their full potential (like all of us are supposed to in our daily jobs). In reality they probably don't want this additional burden. Like the whim of the referee and the width of the crossbar the pro excludes it, counts it as extraneous as he counts the club history. These supporters' obligation is imposed but it is not accepted by the players. Whilst Dunphy was content with that situation at the time he has come to regret the pro's insular view.

"The fans have a much warmer feeling for the club. They're permanent, there before you and after you. It's their club, not yours, You're just there to do a function. You welcome this when you're playing but when you get older, more reflective, you realise you've had a life in sport but you haven't had any relationships outside that life that are really tangible. What you're left with are the personal memories of people you played with, nothing to do with any of the clubs or their supporters."

"There's a shocking sort of vacuum where there should be a relationship but you can explain it in terms of professional hiring and firing of people by directors who are small-time politicians. Amongst the players there's no sentimentality at all. The only old boys' club in football is Manchester United, run by David Sadler who, interestingly, is an ex-amateur."

Then, completely off-the-cuff and very coherently, Dunphy explains the isolation of the professional from the very thing that makes him a professional and gets him talked about.

"The fundamental idea of sport is recreation, socialising, people coming together in a community - that's its raison d'etre. But what you do as a professional footballer inspires in people a desire to play the game and to emulate you. They benefit from the social purposes of sport, go off, meet other people and get something much better out of it than the professional. He just services the transaction and doesn't benefit the way he should from sport. The pro isn't conscious of this irony, nor the irony that he only got into it because he was a fan in the first place."

On the one hand unasked-for devotion, on the other almost masonic insularity and rarely do the twain meet. As a supporter I'd like to know a bit more about what we've been watching. Why the tactics have had to change, why so-and-so's been transfer listed or dropped. Why one or two of them don't seem to be trying.

In his 1986 introduction to 'Only a Game?' Eamon succinctly defended "the good pro" from "the cheats or simple inadequates of other walks of life who come to the Den and apply to our work a set of judgemental criteria they wouldn't have dreamed of applying on a Monday morning. Fuck them."

But all pros aren't necessarily good pros, nor are good pros always good pros every match. Later in the book he writes:

"Dennis knocked a ball up for Hilly on the left wing. Hilly failed to read it and didn't go for it. Dennis put his hands on his hips, head bowed... From then on he played half-heartedly... It was a tight game, and in the early stages we needed all the help, all the geeing up we could get. And there was no-one to do it, Dennis having abdicated."

Millwall fans felt the consequence of Dennis Burnett jacking it in that afternoon even if the cause lay in the manager's office or the boardroom or Gordon Hill's lack of vision.

Are the fans entitled to have a go at him? For the honest pro the intangible rewards of a great football career are enormous, way beyond those available in accountancy or bricklaying. Think of the respect and affection Denis Smith enjoys in the Potteries, Billy Bonds in East London or Charlie Hurley in Sunderland. Steve Bull is building such a reputation in Wolverhampton today. It can all be worth it, if, of course, today's pro considers intangible rewards. Doesn't pay the rent though, I can almost hear Dunphy growl.

Football is several separate worlds and the relationships between these worlds are generally bad. What seems on the face of it to be a fairly simple set of arrangements is beset by vested interests and the differing objectives of the various participants (players, fans, directors, agents, media, commercial people).

Players and fans (and indeed directors) are in the same place at the same time wanting the same thing but the satisfactions they take from it are quite different. And they never talk together about it.

From the club side there is the sound of silence. There are fewer leaks than in politics - not surprising when you consider what happened recently when there was one at Swindon. Interviews with players and managers almost invariably reveal nothing of footballing interest despite asking as many sensible as daft questions.

No-one offers a meaningful manifesto: "This is the kind of club we are, this is where we're going and this is how we aim to get there." It saves thinking and it saves being judged by it, of course.

Journalists, especially at a local level, are not very helpful to supporters. Of necessity they have to protect, and prize where possible, the source of all the information, the club management. Naturally they know a lot more than they will let on in print.

The overwhelming impression is of information management by omerta. Is there a fear that if the fan knew everything that happened in his name ("because the fans are the most important people after all!") he would no longer place his devotion there?

Is it fear of industrial espionage, of rival clubs finding out too much about you? But they'll be the first to know anyway from their contacts inside the game.

Or is it that the difficult business of running a professional football club would become intolerable if clubs were more answerable to their fans? If fans got real answers to the questions they ask each other on the bus or in the pub, would this pose an extra unattainable layer of quality control on the whole apparatus?

What has been written in the past few pages applies to all professional football clubs in general, not just Reading Football Club in particular. Indeed since the Hurley/Waller years the management of the club has undergone a remarkable transformation - at one point with an ex-player becoming the Chairman. Blunders, however, are still made and not fully explained. As an aside on the openness of clubs to debate I wonder if this volume will be sold in the club shop!

So, for the time being, think of football as a system of separate worlds. The players relate to each other, the board talks business with other businessmen, the hooligans stalk each other and the fans talk and occasionally read fanzines that don't fill the information gap.

In an era when there seems more written about what it's like to be a football hooligan rather than a footballer, Eamon Dunphy, even now, is a valuable rarity to the football fan.

He speaks to us directly from that other, far more

fascinating world. What he says may be (but probably isn't) fifteen years out of date and he may not allow us to answer back, but if others follow we may become better educated judges of the pastime we love. We run the risk of disillusionment but devotion, I suspect, will see us back next week.

Are we, players and fans, in it together? Bluntly, the answer is no. Theirs is a short working interlude, ours a lifetime passion. For them the club is a vehicle for livelihood or possibly fame, for us it is an end in itself. The local pro is a pro not a local. As a kid Steve McMahon was an Everton fan and Peter Reid followed Liverpool.

I'm glad to have met Eamon Dunphy the professional footballer and worked with him on this. It's enlightened me about the way footballers work and think. Even if it is the only business in the world where the customer is always wrong!

Pen pictures

Just as a reference, here is a brief resume of the careers of the key players before and after 1975/76. The appearances and goals totals refer to 1975/76 League matches only.

STEVE DEATH

Goalkeeper. Age 26 years; 32 apps; born Ipswich.
Former England Schoolboy International who joined from West Ham in 1970. Went on to make a record 471 appearances before walking out of the club in 1982. Small, agile, brave, generally brilliant, occasionally not.

JOHN TURNER

Goalkeeper. Age 21 years; 14 apps; born Peterlee.
Formerly with Derby, John joined Reading in 1975 and provided good cover for Death. He left for Torquay in 1978 and subsequent improvement brought him a six-figure move to Chesterfield. A shot-stopper who must have learnt to leave his line after he left Elm Park.

GARY PETERS

Right Back. Age 21 years; 25 apps + 5 sub; 2 goals.
Carshalton-born Gary joined from Guildford City in 1975. He won promotion again with Reading in 1979 and moved on to Fulham. He returned as a veteran in 1985 and won a third promotion with Reading. Now in management at Cambridge United. Always enthusiastic, he first became more polished then acquired a sensible appreciation of his abilities and pace.

STEWART HENDERSON

Right Back. Age 28 years; 25 apps + 2 sub; 2 goals.
A Scottish Schoolboy International, signed from Brighton in 1973. Continued in Reading's colours, occasionally in midfield, until 1983 and then became Youth Development Officer. A dogged and thoughtful footballer.

DAVE MORELINE

Left Back. Age 24 years; 44 apps; born Stepney.
Signed from Fulham in 1974, Dave's Reading career was badly affected by injuries but he played on until 1981. Classy but loss of pace forced him to centre-half later.

GEOFF BARKER
Centre Half. Age 26 years; 29 apps + 1 sub; 2 goals.
Geoff played for his home team Hull and Darlington
before signing for Reading in 1975. After his resignation in
1976 he returned six months later and made six further
appearances before joining Grimsby. Craggy and brave.

STEVE HETZKE
Centre-Half. Age 20 years; 17 apps; 1 goal.
Marlborough-born Steve came through the youth team
ranks and went on to make over 250 appearances in a
variety of positions. After winning a second promotion in
1979, he left Elm Park on an odyssey that included
Blackpool, Sunderland, Chester and Colchester. Huge
and powerful. Good shot.

TOMMY YOULDEN
Centre-Half. Age 26 years; 40 apps; 1 goal.
Another Londoner and another England Schoolboy
International, joined Reading from Portsmouth in 1972. He
signed for Aldershot in 1977. Hard and slick defender.

BOBBY LENARDUZZI
Defender. Age 20 years; 13 apps + 3 sub.
A youth team product who returned to his native Canada
in 1976 and represented them in the 1986 World Cup
Finals in Mexico. An energetic but uncertain utility player.

BRYAN CARNABY
Midfield. Age 28 years; 18 apps; 1 goal.
Plymouth-born Bryan was a late developer making his
League debut at 25 in 1972. He retired after the 1977
relegation and was, briefly, the club physio. A wing-half
who desperately wanted to play but never looked very
happy on the pitch. Scored some spectacular goals.

GORDON CUMMING
Midfield. Age 27 years; 30 apps; 1 goal.
A Scot signed as a right winger from Arsenal in 1969
Gordon was the longest-serving member of the team. He
retired in 1978. Slight and skilful, good crosser.

EAMON DUNPHY
Midfield. Age 30 years. 43 apps + 2 sub; 3 goals.
Former Eire international, signed in 1975 from Charlton.
Previous League experience at York and Millwall. Retired
in 1977. Old-style inside-forward and shrewd passer who
"masterminds from a central midfield role", (opposition
programme).

BRUCE STUCKEY
Midfield. Age 28 years. 26 apps; 2 goals.
Joined Reading in 1973 from his home-town team,
Torquay. Previously with Exeter and Sunderland. He
signed for Bournemouth in 1977. A well-built ex-winger
with pace and power rather than guile.

RAY HIRON
Forward. Age 32 years. 42 apps + 1 sub; 11 goals.
Born in Fareham, Ray served nearby Portsmouth for 11
years before joining Reading in 1975. Ray went back to
the Fourth with Reading and ended his days at centre-half
in 1977. A tall, gangling centre-forward, useful in the air
and delicate on the ground.

JACK WHITHAM
Forward. Age 28 years. 17 apps + 6 sub; 3 goals.
Burnley-born Jack was a former England Under 23
International whose career spanned Sheffield
Wednesday, Liverpool and Cardiff. He retired at the end
of this season. Cumbersome, perhaps haunted by past
glories and present injuries.

JOHN MURRAY
**Forward. Age 27 years. 33 apps + 4 sub; 15 goals (5
pens).**
Newcastle-born John had also been in an England Under
23 squad. Formerly with Burnley, Blackpool and Bury, he
signed in 1974 and left Reading in 1978 for Brentford. A
stocky figure with a tremendous shot and good dribbling
skills.

DENNIS NELSON
Forward. Age 25 years. 10 apps; 3 goals.
Dennis was born in Edinburgh and had played for
Dunfermline and Crewe before joining Reading as a pre-
transfer deadline signing in March 1976. He stayed two
seasons before re-joining Crewe. A small, quick and
aggressive forward.

ROBIN FRIDAY
Forward. Age 23 years. 44 apps; 21 goals.
Hammersmith-born Robin was signed from Hayes in 1974
and left Reading for Cardiff in December 1976. In his brief
stay there he helped them to a Welsh Cup Final victory
before walking out on the professional game. Died
Christmas 1990. An inspirational, dribbling centre-forward
who could bring back the old joys of football to the
terraces. Volatile temperament.

OTHER APPEARANCES

Mick Hollis
> Ex-Stockport forward. 4 apps + 3 sub; 1 goal.

Adrian Cooper
> Local boy, ex-Schools International; midfield; 2 apps.

Andy Alleyne
> Youth product; right back; 2 apps.

CHARLIE HURLEY
Manager.
Former Eire international centre-half and captain of Sunderland. Joined Reading as manager in January 1972 and resigned in March 1977.

MAURICE EVANS
Assistant Manager.
Local boy who made over 400 appearances for the club as a player. Formerly manager of Shrewsbury, Maurice took over from Charlie, initially on a caretaker basis. Won Fourth Division Championship in 1979 and Milk Cup with Oxford in 1986 for which he can just about be forgiven.

League playing record 1975-76

Date	Opponent	Venue	Score	Scorers	Attendance
Aug 16	Rochdale	(H)	2-0	Youlden, Hetzke	4,534
23	Crewe Alex.	(A)	3-3	Hiron 2, Friday	2,057
30	Southport	(H)	1-0	Murray	4,595
Sept 6	Lincoln C.	(A)	1-3	Friday	4,327
13	Watford	(H)	3-0	Barker, Murray, Friday	5,521
20	Workington	(A)	2-0	Murray (pen), Friday	1,712
22	Hartlepool	(A)	4-2	Whitham 3, Smith R (og)	2,261
27	Bournemouth	(H)	2-1	Dunphy 2	7,226
Oct 4	Scunthorpe U.	(A)	1-2	Friday	2,177
11	Bradford C.	(H)	2-1	Murray, Hiron	5,885
18	Barnsley	(A)	2-4	Friday, Henderson	2,814
20	Newport Co.	(A)	0-0		2,955
25	Huddersfield T.	(H)	2-0	Cumming, Stuckey	6,679
Nov 1	Doncaster R.	(A)	1-1	Hiron	7,293
5	Swansea C.	(H)	1-0	Murray	5,499
8	Exeter C.	(H)	4-3	Friday, Murray 2 (1 pen), Hiron	6,341
15	Torquay U.	(A)	0-0		2,220
29	Darlington	(A)	1-0	Peters	1,761
Dec 6	Stockport Co.	(H)	5-0	Murray 3, Friday 2	6,701
13	Scunthorpe U.	(H)	1-0	Murray	5,575
19	Tranmere R.	(A)	0-2		3,170
26	Cambridge U.	(H)	1-0	Hiron	7,783
27	Brentford	(A)	2-2	Peters, Stuckey	6,934
Jan 3	Northampton T.	(H)	1-0	Barker	10,139
10	Southport	(A)	2-1	Hiron, Henderson	1,167
17	Workington	(H)	1-0	Friday	7,183
24	Watford	(A)	1-2	Friday	5,944
Feb 6	Swansea C.	(A)	1-5	Friday	2,750
13	Exeter C.	(A)	1-4	Friday	3,641
21	Torquay U.	(H)	0-0		6,259
25	Hartlepool	(H)	1-0	Friday	6,288
28	Huddersfield T.	(A)	0-3		6,546
Mar 2	Newport Co.	(H)	1-0	Murray (pen)	6,211
6	Doncaster R.	(H)	0-1		6,441
13	Bradford C.	(A)	1-1	Nelson	2,916
17	Barnsley	(H)	0-0		6,579
20	Darlington	(H)	4-1	Friday 2, Hollis, Hiron	5,350
26	Stockport Co.	(A)	1-1	Friday	2,319
31	Tranmere R.	(H)	5-0	Murray 3 (2 pens), Friday 2	10,961
Apr 3	Rochdale	(A)	0-0		1,063
7	Bournemouth	(A)	1-0	Nelson	5,372
10	Lincoln C.	(H)	1-1	Hiron	15,683
15	Northampton T.	(A)	1-4	Hiron	3,548
19	Brentford	(H)	1-0	Hiron	12,772
21	Cambridge U.	(A)	2-2	Friday, Carnaby	3,245
24	Crewe Alex.	(H)	3-1	Friday, Dunphy, Nelson	12,229

Additional copies of 'More than a Job?' can be obtained
by sending a cheque for £5.25 per copy, crossed and
made payable to 'Further Thought' to:
Further Thought Publishing
Clumber Cottage
High Street
Upavon
Wiltshire
SN9 6EA